HEAL OR DIE

HEAL OR DIE

Psychotherapists Confront Nuclear Annihilation

Edited by

Kenneth Porter, M.D.

Deborah Rinzler, Ph.D.

Paul Olsen, Ph.D.

The Psychohistory Press
2315 Broadway
New York, New York 10024

HEAL OR DIE: Psychotherapists Confront Nuclear Annihilation

Library of Congress Cataloging-in-Publication Data

Heal or Die.

  Includes bibliographies.
  1. Psychotherapy. 2. Atomic warfare -- Psychological aspects.
3. Adjustment (Psychology) I. Porter, Kenneth, 1943 -
II. Rinzler, Deborah, 1947 -   . III. Olsen, Paul.
RC480.5.H346   1987   616. 89'14   87-20528
ISBN 0-914434-26-8

To my mother and father --
$\qquad$ *--K.P.*

To Cootie-Bug; and to the memories of Kitty-Mama, Ace, and Devil, without all of whom I may never have known anything about it.
$\qquad$ *--D.R.*

To Marissa and Matthew: I tried.
$\qquad$ *--P.O.*

Once more, I sing my little song for closeness to life...--once more, before all is wiped off the grey slate of approaching time, obliterated with a sponge soaked in blood.

--George Grosz

TABLE OF CONTENTS

ACKNOWLEDGMENTS

In thinking back over my anti-nuclear career my thanks go first to my friends in Physicians for Social Responsibility. For over two decades PSR has been at the forefront of the fight to end nuclear fights. I have appreciated the encouragement from PSR in New York City, and especially from Jonathan Lorch, Sid Starkman, and Raoul Rosenberg, who welcomed me into PSR and gave me the opportunity to flower. Harris Peck has also been a friend and support in numerous difficult and rewarding situations over the years. I also have happy memories of time spent with colleagues from across the country in many national meetings of PSR, and think fondly of wonderful trips overseas with the International Physicians for the Prevention of Nuclear War, whose dedication and creativity has inspired me.

My anti-nuclear work began in my teens in Brooklyn with a girl then named Joan Wallach, who first introduced me to the world of radical politics. At Harvard my friends in Tocsin enabled me to enjoy many midnight meetings at which, with Peter Goldmark, Todd Gitlin, Adam Hochschild, Chris Hobson, John Ehrenreich and many others, we boldly planned the future of the world. More recently I am grateful to my colleagues in the Downstate Nuclear Weapons Freeze Campaign, and to Joanna Macy and many others in the Interhelp network who have supported my conviction that love is at the center of anti-nuclear work. Along with these, Bob Lifton has been a model of responsibility and intellectual rigor not excluding humor and humanity.

For the courage to raise the nuclear issue with my patients, I thank those in the past who have stimulated my courage. And lastly my appreciation goes to Deborah and Paul, whose encouragement and friendship throughout all our endeavors have given me the strength I needed when it seemed no strength was left. The idea of this book originated with them.

K.P.

In our commitment to anti-nuclear work, there has been barely a single person who has failed to produce an impact on us, and our full list of acknowledgements might run the length of a small-town telephone directory. Space requirements limit us to deeply and lovingly thank:

Our colleagues at the National Institute for the Psychotherapies who have aided us in a nearly impossible task, especially Patricia Tenerella Brody, Deborah Cotton, and Judith Kurzer, who were present for the work and lived through much more with us; Lucy Hricz, who helped us begin; the Directors of N.I.P., who encouraged and supported N.I.P.'s Nuclear Education Project; Verna D'Alto, who shared both the joy and the despair of our work with us; Harris Peck, inspirational for his patience and tenacity; David Shainberg, who always provides a piece of the energy; Alfreda Galt, who carries on the spirit of Trigant Burrow, a man who knew much of this before most of us were born; and six very special and alive people who provided a searing moment of truth at our *Victim-to Activist* conference: Janet Gordon, Father Dan Berrigan, Setsuko Thurlow, Tom Saffer, Kari Light, and Richard Piccione.

Ken Porter, the third member of **Trinity: The New York Gang,** with our enduring love.

Our clients, who share their lives with us.

And finally Lloyd de Mause, without whom the message of this book might be consigned to oblivion.

D.R. and P.O.

INTRODUCTION

Kenneth Porter, M.D.

A psychotherapist sits in her office with a patient. As the months go by the patient improves. Simultaneously a change occurs in the city around the office. Fires become common, buildings are abandoned. But the therapist is able to continue, and therapy proceeds. Neither patient nor therapist mentions the changes occurring outside the office. Soon the time to terminate arrives. In the closing weeks, the therapist decides to ask why the patient has never discussed the deterioration of the city. Material then emerges of a new and deeper nature. Sessions proceed in an even more fruitful way, until treatment is terminated.

A fantasy? Not at all. For is this not the situation of the psychotherapist in 1987? We conduct psychotherapy; outside, the world is burning.

The danger of nuclear war, the greatest danger ever faced by the human species, confronts the psychotherapist with an unprecedented challenge. Our existence is threatened by an invisible danger we are too frightened or too hopeless to engage. So we reach for security. We follow the rules of our trade. Issues of internal emotional coherence take precedence over issues of external incoherence. Issues must be raised by our patients, not by us. These guidelines protect the therapeutic situation from exploitation by our personal needs, and we can work in a focused and productive way. But outside our offices, the fire rages on.

Ninety years ago one psychotherapist dared ask his patients questions that had always been taboo. Thousands of patients have been the beneficiaries, and have been able to discuss sex normally. But who will be our Freuds today? Who will wrestle with our great taboo—the fear of the end of civilization?

The contributors to this book have dared to face this question. Each following his or her own path, talking with other human beings in a professional situation, each has faced the dread that is shaking the ground of our existence. Of the therapists represented here, some have worked with individual adults, some with families, some with children, some with groups. Some are psychoanalysts, some group therapists, some gestalt therapists. Many different professional disciplines are represented. Some have worked in traditional psychotherapy settings; some have created their own. Some, listening carefully to their patients, have heard references to nuclear war and brought this to their patients' attention. Others have initiated the discussion. Some have focused exclusively on the nuclear issue. For others, it has become part of an expanding process of concern for the integrity of our society, our environment, and the living beings with whom we share our planet.

There is much in this work to be questioned and criticized. We hope for an ongoing dialogue within the mental health profession. We only ask that as these essays are evaluated, they be evaluated in the light of the fire that is raging outside our walls.

For this is not a book of theory. It is a book of practice, of painful, joyful, living practice. These therapists document what they are actually doing, as they struggle with the fear of nuclear war on a daily basis with their patients. This is a report from the front, a report from a few psychotherapists creating a firebreak.

Some will say we are treading where we should not. It is not the role of psychotherapists to introduce political concerns into therapy, some will argue. The therapeutic situation must be shielded from the therapist's own values, no matter how praiseworthy these might be. The patient in psychotherapy, in order to grow, must make himself vulnerable and dependent. Accordingly, he is easily influenced. The autonomy of the patient must be our first concern. Otherwise we undermine the fundamental premise of our work, the belief that, in the proper therapeutic environment, each patient has the capacity to choose his own path for himself far better than anyone else is able to, even his psychotherapist. So it will be argued.

To all of this we respond.

First, nuclear material is already present in our sessions. What prevents it from emerging is our own resistance to confront it.

Second, psychotherapy is interpersonal as well as intra-psychic. We believe that psychotherapy is not only a process occurring within a patient, but also an interpersonal process between patient and psychotherapist, and also a process that occurs in the larger interpersonal context we know as society. Accordingly, valid subjects for psychotherapeutic scrutiny include not only the patient's intra-psychic processes, but also the reality between patient and therapist, and the reality among patient, therapist, and society. To ignore any one of these is to ignore a crucial dimension to the human existence of the patient.

Third, psychotherapy is not value-free. Implicitly our work promotes the values of honesty and human caring, for example, rather than the values of dissembling and destructiveness. Why? We support these values because they are inherent in the process of human growth that is fostered by psychotherapy. We believe the continuity of civilization falls into the same category of values that are an inextricable part of the very process of psychotherapy.

Fourth, psychotherapy is not simply a matter of technique. It requires the engagement of many human aspects of the psychotherapist in addition to technical skill. This includes the thoughtful, disciplined expressions of caring for the future of patients and of ourselves. We do not believe that, in sessions, we are therapists first, and human beings separately. Rather, we believe that to be good psychotherapists, we must be human as part of being therapeutic, and that this entails attention to the threat to our existence.

Fifth and finally, we believe that the psychotherapist at this point in time is in a totally unprecedented situation which changes the rules, and that few as yet have recognized this. Business as usual may mean no business. Radioactive patients will not be amenable to our usual procedures. The continuity of our profession, to say nothing of our own lives, requires we attend to the nuclear threat.

In view of this, we ask that these essays be judged by the broadest of human criteria. The psychoanalyst Erik Erikson has recently said: "We cannot afford to live for long with a division of personal, professional and political ethics." These essays are an attempt to meet this challenge.

Our future as a species may depend upon the ultimate balance in the world between the forces of insightful caring and the forces of blind destructiveness. In this situation, what is the responsibility of the psychotherapist? Are we fulfilling our historic function of daring to ask the questions others fear, in order to liberate the forces of growth within the human personality? Or are we colluding with our patients' fears unknowingly, interpreting their anxieties in the context of old frameworks of thought? Are we avoiding our oldest and primary responsibility—to face the truth and not flinch?

Will life prevail on our planet? Will the danger of nuclear war be quenched by our wisdom and our thoughtful action? We believe it can be, and offer these essays as one attempt to bring some water of understanding to our thirsty planet.

1

The Role of the Psychotherapist in the Nuclear Age

Kenneth Porter, M.D.

> The fateful question for the human species seems to me to be whether and to what extent their cultural development will succeed in mastering the disturbances of their communal life by the human instinct of aggression and self-destruction. It may be that in this respect precisely the present time deserves a special interest. Men have gained control over the forces of nature to such an extent that with their help they would have no difficulty in exterminating one another to the last man. They know this, and hence comes a large part of their current unrest, their unhappiness, and their mood of anxiety. And now it may be expected that the other of the two 'heavenly forces,' eternal Eros, will put forth his strength so as to maintain himself alongside of his equally immortal adversary.[1]
>
> Sigmund Freud, *Civilization and Its Discontents* (concluding words)

All psychotherapy begins with the psychotherapist honestly confronting himself. In this spirit I offer the following observations.

When I was eight I read a comic book which disturbed me. A man was captured on the Earth by aliens who planned to blow up the planet. They injected into the man's bloodstream a substance which would turn him into an atomic bomb in ten days. After being left by the aliens the man tried to tell people. No one would listen and he was told he was crazy.

It took me years to discover the truth of that comic. There is a nuclear bomb inside all of us, our own feelings of hate, that is externalized in the weapons that may kill us. And when we try to warn people, few listen. Occasionally we are called crazy.

In the years since then, I have also learned I am not so different from those who will not listen. As a boy I loved rockets. I loved to sit at my desk and draw pictures of them with crayons. My happiest childhood hours were spent playing imaginary space adventures games with the girl next door (now a computer analyst). I was Steve Strong, captain of the spaceship, she was Joan Dale, and our imaginary companion was Tom Corbett, Space Cadet, which also happened to be the name of the television series from which we took our inspiration. Years later when I joined the peace movement I was still Steve Strong, as I delightedly pored over figures of missiles and warheads, avid as any Pentagon planner, although this time I was "on the other side." But I loved the missiles and I loved the power as much as any strategic thinker.

A PSYCHOLOGICAL UNDERSTANDING
OF THE NUCLEAR SITUATION

In my opinion our country, and all countries with nuclear weapon, are ill. The illness is not our desires to hate and to achieve supreme power. These are just the facts of our humanity. The illness consists of our acting these feelings out.

These feelings that we all find within us—wishes to be destructive and desires for supreme magical power—form the psychological core of the nuclear problem. Nuclear weapons are an externalization of these historic, deep-seated urges, present in all humankind since the beginning of civilization, unchecked by our normal fear of death. Any one of us who takes the time and effort to look within can discover these urges.

Therefore, nuclear weapons are our weapons. We have dreamed them. We have built them. We have deployed them. And we are getting ready to use them.

The strange thing about us as human beings is that we are both animal and mind at the same time. As was said in the Middle Ages, we are half animals and half angels. The glory of homo sapiens—mind—is two-faced. It can look outward, and, transcending the present and the body, can remember history, can imagine the future. So we talk, write and build civilization. But our glory can betray us. In being able to transcend ourselves, we can also ignore ourselves. We can deny we are animals. We can forget we want to kill. And when impulses go unacknowledged, they can be acted out, regardless of consequences. What is unacknowledged cannot be controlled.

Today our species has lost contact with the fact that we are not *separate* from nature; we *are* nature. In forgetting that we are animals, we are becoming guilty of the greatest sin of all. This is the sin of playing God. Watching the first test of the atomic weapon he created, the most powerful force ever to exist in the history of the planet, Robert Oppenheimer found himself struck by the famous lines from the Bhagavad-Gita, uttered by Vishnu:

> 'Behold, now I am become Death,
> Shatterer of Worlds.'[2]

How have we allowed this unprecedented situation to come about?

Intra-psychic defenses, large group processes and cultural historical attitudes have all converged to produce our nuclear dilemma.

INTRA-PSYCHIC DEFENSES

First, the very nature of nuclear anxiety—the fear that our friends and family and civilization may die in addition to us—is a new anxiety in the history of humanity. It arouses the deepest fears of our childhood, of the symbiotic time when we and the world were one, and so a disturbance in the world felt like an inner, unendurable catastrophe.[3]

Second, we have employed a number of intra-psychic defenses to avoid our nuclear anxiety. These include the following familiar refuges from reality.

1. *Denial* ("I just don't want to think about it.")

2. *Nuclear numbing.* This is a complex of defensive operations, aptly named by psychiatrist Robert Lifton.[4] It consists of a particular deadening of internal emotional life, such that emotional responsiveness to multiple aspects of human experience, in addition to the nuclear threat, is blunted, in order to spare an individual the intense emotional pain of confronting the danger of nuclear war.

3. *Isolation of affect.* Former nuclear war planner Roger Molander tells the story of a Navy captain who objected to excitement about the consequences of nuclear war. The captain stated, "only 500 million people would be killed."[5]

4. *Fantasies of omnipotent control* of the outside world. This is reflected in obsessive counting of warheads and missiles, and in fantasies that nuclear war can be limited.

5. *Regression to passivity.* The knowledge, judgment and skill of political leaders is over-estimated, in order to produce the illusion that we are being taken care of by wise, loving parent-figures. The corresponding abilities of the ordinary citizen are denigrated.

6. *Fixation*. Most military planners have not given up outmoded military concepts of the past ("winning," "national security"). They do not see that the advent of nuclear weapons has radically changed military theory, which now requires not winning but preventing, not making weapons but unmaking them, and not national security but global security.

7. *Projection*. The problem is said not to be a common problem, with a portion of the responsibility resting with us. Rather, it is "the Russians' fault."

8. *Defensive grandiosity*. Some individuals block out their fear of nuclear weapons by identifying with them. In technical terms, the individual fuses his primitive idealized self with the powerful external object of the bomb, obtains an illusion of sadistic omnipotence, and feels safer. This phenomenon has been labelled by Lifton "nuclearism."[6]

9. *The experience of powerlessness as a defense*. Powerlessness is defensive in three ways. First, it ignores important aspects of reality. Recent American history (the nuclear testing protests of the fifties and the Vietnam protests of the sixties) show that public opinion can affect public policy. Second, feeling powerlessness can lead to "giving up," which can be a way to avoid the anxiety of trying to prevent nuclear war when we are not sure we can. Third, powerlessness is often a reaction to our own grandiosity. The nuclear threat is so awful we respond with a fantasy of an omnipotent solution. Only an immensely effective act is worth undertaking. When this fantasy collapses we are left feeling powerless. In fact not our powerlessness, but only our powerlessness to change the world overnight, has been demonstrated.

On the next level, nuclear anxiety is also avoided by what might be called large-group defenses. These include splitting, grandiosity and projection on a social scale.

LARGE-GROUP DEFENSES AND CULTURAL ATTITUDES

Within the United States, subgroups have formed to deal with the nuclear threat. One group is anti-nuclear, another is pro-defense. Each considers that it is all-good, and that the other is all-bad. In more technical terms, each group projects its internal feelings of destructiveness onto the other group. Each group also has a representation of itself as perfect. We therefore have two groups facing each other in political conflict, claiming that they differ radically, which are actually quite similar psychologically. Neither can face clearly and deal constructively with its own conviction of perfection, and its own internal feelings of anger, without getting arrogant and blaming someone else.

A similar process goes on at an international level. The citizens of each super-power have a self-representation of their country as all-good, and an object representation of the opposing country as all-bad. Sometimes the situation is more complex, and a split develops in our mental representation of the opposing side. We see the "people" of the Soviet Union, for example, as "good," but the "leaders" are bad. Having visited in the Soviet Union recently and talked with both their "leaders" and "people" I can report they make a similar distinction about the United States.

This leads to an interactive cycle that, like all systems, homeostatically resists change. Each system projects its own internal badness on the other, then becomes afraid of the other, reacts angrily, provokes aggression in the opponent, and then feels more afraid. Since the process of splitting and projection remains unconscious, we remain unaware it is our *own* feelings of hate and grandiosity we are projecting. Hence we can securely act these feelings out, convinced that we are responding to the other side, and unconscious of our own profound fear of dying. The other side does the same, and, like a marital couple in tortured love, we cannot grow but remain trapped and stabilized.

A third level in society, cultural values, supports this. Since the Renaissance, we in Western civilization have emphasized certain aspects of experience and minimized others. We have emphasized those aspects associated with our concept of manhood: controlling nature; being powerful; being competitive; making material progress; and being intellectual. We have minimized aspects of life associated for us with being a woman: being a part of nature; being nurturing; being cooperative; being itself; and being sensual and emotional.

Nuclear weapons are the ultimate, inevitable expression of the hypertrophy of masculine principles in Western culture. This is the principle that the controlled use of destructive power in a competitive situation for material ends should receive primacy in our lives. As a result, our culture is like a teenager who has just discovered drugs and fast cars. We are tearing down the highway at 100 miles an hour, oblivious to the dangers, aware only of our excitement. With nuclear power we are discovering the incredible thrill of thinking we can control unbelievable forces of nature.

I do not believe there is any way we can say that all these historical and psychological developments have been negative. For one thing they were probably unpredictable and unavoidable. Just as in a human life so it is in human history: we do what we need to do, and if it becomes apparent we have acted unwisely, then we try to make the necessary corrections.

Moreover, the gains for the West, and for humankind in general, from this historical process, have been enormous. These have included, to name just a few, the development of reason as a force in intellectual history; the freedom from bondage to religious tradition just for tradition's sake; the development of nation-states and of political liberty and democracy; individualism; the development of science, technology, industrialism and the age of information; enormous economic gains for millions of our planet's inhabitants.

Even within the major cultures of the West, psychological polarization into opposing nation-states has not been without benefit. We have clarified the distinction between "our" society and "theirs," and thereby consolidated feelings of national identity. Friendly feelings within each society have been increased, since disruptive anger has been directed outwards. And since leaders have been idealized, most populations have felt taken care of by wise, loving parents.

However, the cost has also been enormous. The acting-out of hate and grandiosity without full awareness has potentially catastrophic consequences. And this acting-out has been facilitated by the anonymity and resulting lack of individual responsibility that attends all large-group processes, including those on the historical stage.

Thus the question is not whether these directions were mistakes, but whether humankind will now reach its maturity. Will we master our aggressiveness and become adults, or will we remain thrill-seeking, power-hungry adolescents and crack ourselves up? Indeed, all issues facing our species in the 21st century—the nuclear issue, the preservation of the ecosphere, the problem of hunger and the larger conflict between North and South—all partake of the need for humankind to master its impulses.

In searching for ways in which this may be accomplished, it is important to note that the slice of life that we in the West have chosen to emphasize is only one of many possible alternatives. Many Eastern cultures have chosen other approaches, which is what has led many to suggest that what is needed is not an abandonment of Western, or so-called "masculine" principles, but a union of these with the more traditionally Eastern, or "feminine" approaches.

In this connection it is instructive to note that even within Western civilization there is a strong trend warning against the abuse of power. The great mythic heroes (all, not accidentally, male) have been Phaeton, Icarus, Oedipus, Prometheus, Adam, Faustus and Ahab. All have exhibited the sin of hubris, that is, the danger of acting-out great power without self-knowledge.

Phaeton, the son of Apollo, drove the chariot of the sun that only his father should have driven, scorched the earth, and was destroyed. Icarus, seeking ever-greater heights of technological supremacy, flew too close to the sun and was killed. Oedipus, achieving power without self-knowledge, brought drought and destruction on his land, until he himself was willing to look within, gain awareness, and make corrections. Prometheus, the God who gave humankind science and technology through fire, overstepped his natural limits and was punished.

Adam and Eve gained knowledge without morality and lost their paradise. Faustus sold his soul to the devil for power and paid the heavy price. Ahab projected all evil on the Soviet Union of his time, a white mammal, sacrificed all to eradicate it in his search for supreme power, and sacrificed himself. Closer to us, in one of the most popular epics of our time, Tolkien has pointed out that there are certain powers, like certain rings, that are too dangerous ever to use, and that must be destroyed, not employed.

It is also of interest that the single most influential idea in the history of Western civilization, the Crucifixion, symbolizes the pursuit of the opposite course, the willingness to renounce power for the sake of love.

WHAT CAN THE PSYCHOTHERAPIST DO
TO PREVENT NUCLEAR WAR?

Faced with this situation, what is the role of the psychotherapist in the nuclear age?

In times of social crisis, certain groups in society feel most acutely the danger to all. Through self-exploration and self-expression, they serve as prophets or beacons to the rest of us, to lead us out of our darkness.

In former years, miners of coal were often faced with a difficulty. Working at risk of their lives deep underground, they faced sudden death from an invisible but lethal threat—deadly gas. They devised a plan, an early warning plan, so to speak, to inform them of imminent danger before it might be too late. Down to their mines they carried caged canaries, terribly sensitive to toxic fumes. When their canaries became affected, they knew it was time to act.

Who are our caged canaries, desperately trying to warn us? Let us listen.

> A girl, aged 12: "One lady, a doctor, in a film said that it was our responsibility to carry on our great life cycle. She said it was up to us to make sure that all of our knowledge, our achievements, the art and our culture are preserved. This brought tears to my eyes. It hit me. This is not a joke or something to not worry about. I face in my lifetime the power to destroy a living race that took billions of years to evolve. We are playing God with a world that does not belong to us alone."[7]

> A boy, aged 18: "I went to a conference on nuclear power a while back. At least fifty people stood and talked about the horrors of a nuclear war. However, through all the talk of the scientists, and experts, and religious leaders, and political

leaders, I kept thinking, 'What about us? What about the generation that really has to live with this fear?' Then an eleventh-grader from Plymouth, Mass. got up and with a shaking voice explained to about three hundred adults what it feels like to have your whole life set-up based on the fear that the world just might not be around for you to grow up in. He said, 'No one should have the right to choose whether an entire generation gets to grow up or not.' What can possibly be more simple? No one has that right.''[8]

Two organizers of the Children's Campaign for Nuclear Disarmament: "The question is, are the adults of the world protecting us? The answer to that is, no." "We feel that the world we are being given is broken."[9]

Today the psychotherapist, if he chooses, can join the world's children in serving as the planet's caged canaries.

What will this require?

First, honest self-exploration.

Second, like the children, we must sing. We must offer our expertise to society. For we know more than we sometimes let on about how people change—it is our business, after all. Part of the reason for our current hopelessness about the nuclear situation is that we are not applying the professional knowledge we already do have to the nuclear arena. If we do so, I believe we will see that many factors are already in place that augur well for the future.

Third, we should deal with the nuclear issue in our practice of psychotherapy.

A SYSTEMS THEORY OF GROWTH AND IMPLICATIONS FOR POLITICAL ACTIVISM

About three years ago I had been asked so many times by the anti-nuclear movement to say something about what I knew as a psychiatrist that was relevant to anti-nuclear work, that I sat down and thought, what do we know about personal change in psychotherapy that is relevant to political change? I came to the conclusion that the process of human growth may be similar in many areas of human endeavor. Scientific invention, artistic creativity, psychotherapeutic change, political revolution, biological evolution, the human birth process and spiritual transformation may all be more similar than we have realized.

What does it take for a patient in psychotherapy to change? You have to recognize there is a problem. You have to accept responsibility for it. You have to have motivation to change it. You have to have an alter-

native. You have to have hope. You need support. And you have to overcome resistance. These conditions for change—recognition, responsibility, motivation, alternative, hope, support and resistance—are also key to
political change. This understanding can be shared by psychotherapists
with those sectors of society seeking change.

I would like to emphasize three particular aspects of the change process. These are motivation, and especially fear; the role of resistance and
impasse; and current possibilities for hope.

Fear is a great motivator. But we have learned a great deal about fear
or anxiety in our work as psychotherapists. Fear should be optimal, not
maximal, to produce constructive effects. Too little fear stifles. But too
much fear paralyzes. This is important information for political activists.

The creative role of impasse is not appreciated in the nuclear situation.
As psychotherapists we know that resistance regularly precedes progress.
Scientists and artists know that total blockage regularly precedes creative
breakthrough. Political revolutionaries know that misery precedes
upheaval. Biologists now tell us that ecological crisis can lead to radical,
discontinuous species-change that breaks the usual slow evolutionary
pattern. And the spiritual traditions of all cultures have told us for millenia that death must precede re-birth.

We are creatures of habit. No one gives birth by choice. Only when we
are totally convinced that the old ways are useless will we be willing to die
and, under the pressure of the crisis, recoil into ourselves, plunge
through the cracking layers of our conscious selves, and contact our
deeper, regressive sources of creativity in order to give birth to the new.
Understood in this way, what Joanna Macy and others have dared to
say, which at first seems so shocking, may indeed be true, that the bomb
may be a gift. It may be the gift we give ourselves to help us find the
energy for the new social changes we need to survive as a species in a
more fulfilled way.

Hope is a missing ingredient in the nuclear equation. We cannot
change in treatment without hope, no matter how great the pain or how
deep the insight. Even political revolutions, though fuelled by suffering,
only occur during times of relief. Despair sets the stage, then must be
softened by hope to emerge into creative action.

Feelings of hopelessness about our nuclear situation arise when our
objective knowledge about the possibilities for constructive social change
is overwhelmed by our nuclear anxiety. The intensity of nuclear anxiety
itself sometimes interferes with cognitive functioning. Therefore it is
useful for those knowledgeable in human behavior to remind themselves,
and others, of the facts of political opportunity.

Historically, effective social change has often been initiated not by a
majority of the members of a society, but by a committed minority. This
important fact reminds us that the possibilities for change in the nuclear

situation may be greater than we allow. It is illustrated by the charming and well-known story of the "hundredth monkey." In the 1950's a group of monkeys on an island in the Pacific were under study. Apparently the monkeys ate their sweet potatoes in the sand, until one young girl monkey was observed to discover the idea of washing the potato in water to improve the taste. The idea gradually spread among other monkeys. The question is, how did the idea make progress through the colony? Was it a simple linear progression? What was observed was that after a sufficiently large minority group of the monkeys got the idea (hypothetically named "the first hundred monkeys"), the remainder suddenly caught on to the idea like wildfire. In short, effective social change may require not a convinced majority but a dedicated, and much more easily achievable, minority. And any one of us might be the decisive "hundredth monkey" to tip the scale.[10]

Another source for hope in the current situation arises from recent findings in the field of biological evolution. New thinking among biologists suggests that evolutionary change may be of two kinds: slow, linear, quantitative change, and rapid, discontinuous, jumps. Evidently when the ecological need is great enough, or when social stress is sufficiently intense, major species change can occur suddenly. It is possible that this could be the situation that our species faces now with regard to its nuclear future.[11]

Finally, it is important to remind ourselves of those major social changes that our species has accomplished over recent millenia. Agriculture, writing and cities were invented. Major social institutions that once seemed immutable, such as human sacrifice, human slavery and male political hegemony, have changed significantly. And in this regard it may be important that some historians believe that war itself as a social institution may only be 15,000 years old—less than 1% of our lifetime as a species.

On a social level, therefore, therapists should use their knowledge to help citizens outside of therapy come to grips with their nuclear feelings. We say that groups are ideal arenas for confronting splitting and projection, fear, shame and isolation. Why not use constructively-led group experiences to facilitate the reowning of those split-off feelings of rage and grandiosity whose denial fuels our current nuclear fire? The hundreds of experiential nuclear workshops known as "despair and empowerment workshops," conducted in North America and Europe for the last decade for over 20,000 people, are one attempt.[12]

Between nations, group and family systems thinking can aid conflict resolution. The little-publicized organization Moral Rearmament played a crucial role in facilitating the emergence of the African state of Zimbabwe; the Harvard University arms and conflict resolution study group may play a similar role in coming years.[13]

In addition, psychotherapists can play a crucial role as citizens, in daily public contact with friends and colleagues. By training and experience, when we are in the public arena, we are able to bear certain otherwise difficult emotional experiences without needing to deny, project or act them out. For better or worse, we are still, despite jokes and insults, the recipients of society's wishes for wisdom and leadership. This role, which we enjoy, benefit from, and suffer from, brings with it the opportunity to serve as containers, or role-models, for others in our discussion of this issue.

CLINICAL EXPLORATIONS

Moved by these speculations, in the spring of 1982 I decided to introduce the subject of nuclear war into my practice of individual and group psychoanalytic psychotherapy. I gave copies of the then-recently published *Fate of the Earth,* by Jonathan Schell,[14] to about 90% of my patients as presents, and suggested they read them. I handed the book out to patients and groups at the beginning of their sessions, and then initiated a discussion of the subject with them. The range of patients was from neurotic to borderline diagnostically, and the range of treatment modality was from five times weekly analytic treatment on the couch to once-weekly supportive psychotherapy. On clinical grounds I excluded about 10% of my patients from the procedure. I gave the book as a gift to dramatically highlight the issue and to facilitate the chances that patients would actually read the book and take the subject seriously.

What were the effects of this unorthodox psychotherapeutic behavior on the treatment situation?

What I did had some effect on patients' attitudes and behavior. After three to six months about two-thirds of patients had read the book, and about one-third stated the nuclear issue had started to affect them more in their daily lives. Two or three initiated major anti-nuclear projects.

Clinically, treatment proceeded. Most patients discussed the issue briefly and then returned to dealing with the other issues of their lives. About 20% of patients had strong reactions, usually an intensification of their previous pattern of transference, either positive or negative. These either consisted of strong feelings of appreciation, and wanting to undertake anti-nuclear work, or strong feelings of resentment to me, feeling I was using my professional position to control them. I dealt with these reactions as I would any other reactions in treatment, listening, trying to understand and reacting in whatever way seemed most constructive to the patients' growth. At times this even included pointing out to patients that they were talking about the nuclear issue to obtain my approval or to avoid dealing with other important issues in their lives.

Why did I take this entire unorthodox action as a psychotherapist?

I did this because, in the final analysis, I found I could not live with myself if I did not. I did it because, although it certainly was not psychoanalytic procedure, I began to realize that no one was talking about the subject anywhere. It was hardly correct legal technique for an attorney to bring this up with his client, hardly appropriate for the cleaner to discuss it with his customers, hardly feasible to disrupt a family dinner to talk about it with your loved ones—so I began to suspect that no time was the right time and no place was the right place, that we were all using rules as obsessional defenses against being full human beings. Ultimately I brought it up because I do not consider myself "a psychotherapist" but "a human being who happens to practice psychotherapy," and it seemed a disservice to my patients and myself to pretend otherwise. After all, if the bomb falls and I happen to be lucky enough to survive, I do not intend to be in the position of explaining to my future children that I never discussed the subject during working hours because it was not considered good technique.

I recently discussed this with an analyst who is a very committed man in work on nuclear issues. I asked, suppose you had a completed analysis and the patient never once mentioned nuclear war? Would you bring it up yourself? I said, how could someone go through an analysis and not bring up sex, not bring up their parents, not bring this issue up? Wouldn't you say, about this too, "You know it's very interesting that you've been lying here for 500 hours and never once mentioned your father, or never once mentioned nuclear war?" He said to me, it would disturb the transference situation—which of course indeed it would. I said in response, but isn't there something else that might happen that would disturb the transference situation even more?

Many therapists are not comfortable with the position I am taking—that the therapist should introduce the subject of nuclear issues into the treatment if the patient does not—but instead are starting to pay more attention to *patients'* references to it. They are starting to report that as they have resolved some of their own inner resistances to dealing with the nuclear threat, they have been surprised to find many more covert nuclear references in their patients' material than they had realized were there. And picking up these references has enhanced and deepened the treatment.

As therapists, therefore, we need to be more sensitive to nuclear issues in our patients. We know that children, teenagers and adults are troubled by nuclear fears, but say they have no place to go with them. Are we hearing this, latent in our patients' communications? Are we picking it up, empathically responding, and facilitating the constructive verbal expression of the fear, grief and rage within the sessions? Are we even hearing *direct* nuclear references, or are we dealing with them as derivatives of purely intra-psychic conflicts?

How many physicians one hundred years ago dared not ask their patients about sex, and explained that their patients simply did not bring it up? Then one courageous individual dared cross the dreaded line and broke the taboo. We have all been the beneficiaries. But who will be our Freuds today? Who will help us confront, in psychotherapy, what is today the greatest taboo of all—the fear of talking about the nuclear threat?

We are very privileged individuals at this time in the history of the world, incredibly privileged. We are also extremely fortunate. We have very important skills that are in need. Who else can bear these feelings that we are asking ourselves to bear? Who else can admit that he does not care sometimes, that he wants to kill, that he feels like giving up, that he feels frightened for his life? Who else will have the courage to do this publicly, to really get up and name the unnameable?

We emerge from a long and very honorable tradition. No human being can fully bear his or her own feelings. None of us can fully tolerate ourselves. None of us can fully tolerate looking at the reality of our own existence. So a long time ago society decided to designate certain people to be the carriers of the unnameable truth. And those certain people would be the people who would be able to name the unnameable. Medicine men, witch doctors, shamans, oracles, diviners, healers, psychotherapists, gurus. For whatever the personal reasons, we are the inheritors of that tradition. We are the ones to bear the feelings of other people that cannot be beared by them, to metabolize the feelings within ourselves, and to constantly pursue the project of helping others re-own their feelings, giving them back their feelings in a way they can tolerate, so that they can heal themselves and get a greater feeling of inner peace. And since we, of course, are none other than part of the same society, every time we heal them a little, we go through the same healing process ourselves.

Thinking along these lines, Carl Jung ventured the thought that our only chance as a civilization to avoid the nuclear holocaust might be if enough individuals could stand the tension of opposites within themselves.[15]

At this stage of history, therefore, our responsibility as psychotherapists has never been greater. But our opportunity has never been greater. I believe that if we avoid this task we will be forever burdened with guilt. Not just guilt toward others, but also the guilt of self-denial, the guilt of not letting ourselves feel who we really are, fully. But we need to act not just to avoid guilt. The fulfillment of our task brings with it our own self-acceptance, the opportunity to be more in touch with our own feelings, the opportunity to be more fully human, and the opportunity to be more fully in contact with each other, so that there can be more joy in our lives.

One from whom we have learned much in recent decades, Erik Erikson, said not long ago: "We cannot afford to live for long with a division of personal, professional and political ethics."[16] Who will begin to heal this division?

> If I am not for myself, who will be for me?
> If I am only for myself, what am I?
> If not now, when?

FOOTNOTES

1. Sigmund Freud, *Civilization and Its Discontents.* N.Y.: Doubleday Anchor Books, 1958, p. 105.
2. Robert Oppenheimer, quoted in Robert Jay Lifton, *The Broken Connection.* N.Y.: Simon and Schuster, 1979, p. 370.
3. Jane E. Pearce, "Terror/Apathy/Nuclear War." In *American Journal of Social Psychiatry.* Vol. 3. Winter, 1983, p. 5-14.
4. Robert Jay Lifton and Richard Falk, *Indefensible Weapons: The Political and Psychological Case Against Nuclearism.* N.Y.: Basic Books, 1982.
5. Roger Molander, "How I Learned to Start Worrying and Hate the Bomb," *Washington Post,* March 21, 1982, p. D5.
6. Robert Jay Lifton, *The Broken Connection.* N.Y.: Simon and Schuster, 1979.
7. Quoted in Vivienne Verdon-Roe, "Growing Up in the Nuclear Age." In *East West Journal,* January, 1983, p. 29.
8. Quoted in John E. Mack, "The Perception of U.S.-Soviet Intentions and Other Psychological Dimensions of the Nuclear Arms Race." In *Preparing for Nuclear War: The Psychological Effects.* N.Y.: Physicians for Social Responsibility/NYC, 1982, p. 22.
9. *Children's Campaign for Nuclear Disarmament,* Box 550, RFD #1, Plainfield, Vermont 05667.
10. Ken Keyes, *The Hundredth Monkey,* St. Mary, Kentucky: Vision Books, 1981.
11. Stephen Jay Gould, quoted in Marilyn Ferguson, *The Aquarian Conspiracy.* Los Angeles: J.P. Tarcher, 1980, p. 158-160.
12. Joanna Rogers Macy, *Despair and Personal Power in the Nuclear Age.* Philadelphia: New Society, 1983.
13. William D. Davidson and Joseph V. Montville, "Foreign Policy According to Freud." In *Foreign Policy,* Vol. 45, Winter, 1981-1982.
14. Jonathan Schell, *The Fate of the Earth.* N.Y.: Knopf, 1982.
15. Quoted in B. Hannah, *Encounter with the Soul.* Santa Monica, CA: Sigo Press, 1981, p. 8.
16. Quoted in Margaret Brenman-Gibson, "Erik Erikson and the 'Ethics of Survival.'" In *Harvard Magazine,* November-December, 1984, p. 61.

2

Addressing the Nuclear Issue in the Psychotherapy Hour: A Clinical and Personal Perspective

Ellen Becker, M.A.

Recently, a client mentioned that we would be meeting on her birthday on Tuesday, August 6. She would be forty. She was going to celebrate with friends at a restaurant in San Francisco. She said that each year she feels a pull to celebrate her own birth and life and acknowledge the tragedy that occurred just hours before her birth. "Here I am celebrating forty years of life on this earth and just a few hours before I was born over 70,000 people were killed, vaporized almost instantly or died slowly and painfully in an event that would draw World War II to a close and end an age of innocence for our planet. Every year it seems I must do something to acknowledge this event on my birthday but this year it feels even more poignant and powerful." She wondered about other people who were born on August 6th of that year and how they handled the associations and enormity of that day in history. She thought about how it must have been for her mother who heard about the bombing as she labored to give birth to her infant.

Living under that shadow of the nuclear peril has affected us all. We may choose to employ denial. We may hope that we are at the epicenter when the bomb is dropped. We may examine the effects of living in the Nuclear Age. As Jonathan Schell says:

> The choice is really between two entirely different ways of
> life. One response is to decline to face the peril, and thus go

on piling up the instruments of doom year after year until, by accident or design, they go off. The other response is to recognize the peril, dismantle the weapons, and arrange the political affairs of the earth so that the weapons will not be built again...we do not have two earths at our disposal—one for experimental holocausts and the other to live on.[1]

In this paper, I will discuss various ways that the nuclear issue can and does enter the clinical hour. Through the use of vignettes and two case histories I will examine the implications of working with the nuclear issue both on a content level as well as intrapsychically, and finally, I will address the transference and countertransference involved in dealing with the global crisis.

Nuclear war is infinitely horrible and difficult to imagine. It seems we must struggle with our concept of history and what is unimaginable if we are to make sense of how we are afflicted by the times we live in. There were over 75,000 people killed within the first hour of dropping the A-Bomb on Hiroshima. 75,000 more deaths were reported within a few months. Hibakusha or A-Bomb Victims continue to die today from exposure to radiation in 1945. Hibakusha literally means explosion-affected person. Judith Lifton, M.D., says we are all explosion-affected people with our own brand of psychic numbing.[2] In spite of the fact that a single weapon today equals one thousand Hiroshimas, we choose to reject the experience of Hiroshima and Nagasaki as historical realities and as a warning for our future. We are numb to the nuclear arms race and our own peril.

For example, living in the Bay Area with missiles pointed at us, submarines off our coast, nuclear materials being transported from one military or scientific installation to another—Livermore National Weapons Laboratories, Concord Naval Weapons Station and Alameda Naval Air Base—we close our eyes. It's difficult to imagine that something we can't see, taste, smell, or touch can be so threatening. The information we receive from the Federal Government tells us a nuclear war is survivable, limited nuclear war is probable, continued nuclear proliferation and nuclear superiority are the only way to insure our nation's safety, while scenarios of nuclear winter and the realistic damages to Hiroshima and Nagasaki and their survivors assault our awareness. How do we assimilate such divergent beliefs?

The mushroom cloud, the pillar of fire, nuclear winter and nuclear annihilation have penetrated deeply into our consciousness through the media. Recent covers of *Time* and *Newsweek;* articles in *The Nation, The New Yorker,* and *Ladies Home Journal;* daily newspaper reporting on arms talks; films and television coverage like *Testament, War Games, Mad Max: Beyond Thunderdome, Threads,* and recent episodes of

"Fame" and "St. Elsewhere" contribute to our awareness of the issue. Paul Brians reported in *The New York Times* that Americans have begun to accept the reality and survivability of a nuclear holocaust.[3] Either we deny the reality of the nuclear peril or we reconcile ourselves to the inevitability of a nuclear war. Neither choice is acceptable.

These images arouse doubts about our future, future generations and the fate of the earth. Research by John Mack,[4] Sibylle Escalona,[5] and Benina Berger-Gould and the Nuclear Ecological Research Project,[6] found that seventy percent of those surveyed were fearful of the possibility of a nuclear holocaust in their lifetime. The level of concern has stretched over class boundaries. In a recent survey by Scott Hass in Manchester, New Hampshire, a surprisingly large percentage of working class students saw nuclear war as inevitable.[7] It seems that nuclear fear has crept into our consciousness. One of the tasks we face as psychotherapists is to assist our clients in assimilating, understanding, and coping with unpleasant, unthinkable images from external reality that cause pain, despair, sadness, and fear. When images which arise out of our experience of reality are not integrated into our lives, they affect the nature of reality. Yet, as psychotherapists, we are timid about responding to the clues we hear from our clients. At best, the references to the nuclear issue are interpreted intrapsychically. At worst, we ignore them. If we are to aid our clients in dealing with their sense of peril and helplessness, we clinicians must face our own inhibitions about the nuclear peril.

In general, denial can be an appropriate defense mechanism against sources of anxiety and stress. Both denial and numbing are accepted stages in the grieving process.[8] They enable us to absorb the reality of the loss of a loved one gradually. Denial also allows us to accomplish tasks that may be necessary in the early stages of a mourning process. But even in the grieving process, denial and numbing that continue over long periods of time can be symptomatic of pathological grief. It can affect our ability to function. It can incapacitate us physically. Our emotions may become deadened or impaired. Our relationships may suffer. As psychologists, we know the importantce of denial as an appropriate defense mechanism. In relation to the nuclear conflict, our mass denial seems dangerous.

Post-traumatic stress disorder is defined in the American Psychiatric Association's Diagnostic and Statistical Manual of Mental Disorders, Third Edition (DSM III) as the development of characteristic symptoms following a psychologically traumatic event that is generally outside the range of usual human experience. This disorder can be found in people of any age who suffer from traumatic events and display alternating cycles of intrusive and avoidant symptoms.[9] The intrusive phase of post-traumatic stress disorder is marked by a variety of interconnected symptoms. Sudden intense waves of emotion may well up uncontrollably, stimulated by seemingly innocent everyday details. Intrusive images and thoughts about the traumatic event may force themselves into consciousness and prove difficult to dispel. Nightmares and unpleasant fantasies connected with the event may also occur. By contrast, the avoidant phase of post-traumatic stress disorder is characterized by an inner sense of numbness. This narrowing of attention facilitates the avoidance of associational connections that might evoke the traumatic event. Avoidance sometimes takes the form of withdrawal.

Although post-traumatic stress disorder is usually diagnosed after events suffered by individuals, it can be stated that our society as a whole has responded to the nuclear threat with a collective stress response syndrome. The psychological unreality of the nuclear peril supports the human tendency to ignore emotionally upsetting information. Societal annihilation is unthinkable. Jonathan Schell:

> Before long, denial of reality becomes a habit—a dominant mode in the life of society—and unresponsiveness becomes a way of life. The society that has accepted the threat of its utter destruction soon finds it's hard to react to lesser ills, for a society cannot be at the same time asleep and awake, insane and sane, against life and for life.[10]

Avoidance may take various forms: denial that there is a problem, denial of the possibility of nuclear accidents or repression of memories of instances where nuclear war almost occurred. The intrusive phase can be found in the dream images evoked in children, adolescents and adults and the intense emotionalism that emerges when one faces the global peril as we live on the edge of extinction. This combination of an all-pervasive concern plus an inability to think about the problem is characteristic of stress response syndrome. The exploding of the atomic bomb has served as a collective trauma whose meaning we have been unable to absorb. It is too painful to think about and too frightful to avoid.

About three and a half years ago, I became involved in establishing an organization in the Bay Area, Psychotherapists for Social Responsibility. I had been politically involved and it felt important to see if I could combine my skills as a psychotherapist with my political and social concerns. I had a desire to confront my own feelings of numbing and despair concerning an escalating arms race, its socio-political ramifications and the environmental and ecological devastation of the earth. A training group for members of Psychotherapists for Social Responsibility was organized wherein we explored our reaction to the peril and our fear regarding a nuclear holocaust. This kind of exercise allowed me to feel my pain for the world and the interconnectedness of all life. It was empowering to face my darkest feelings and know that other people shared the pain and grief. The mutually felt desire to mobilize and empower ourselves to struggle together and to wrestle with the possible extinction of our planet was supportive. It was important to witness other colleagues confront their own denial and numbing.

At that time, I was unwilling to address these issues with my clients. I work psychodynamically as a clinician, blending object relations with Jungian work. I do long-term psychotherapy. I felt my strong reactions to the nuclear issue were my own and did not want to impose them in the clinical hour. I needed to address the depth of my reactions to this peril in my own analysis and with my affinity group made up of colleagues who had participated in the training group. Many of us spoke up quite forcibly, advocating not dealing with the nuclear issue in the clinical hour.

About one year later, my position shifted considerably. That year was spent in examining my own despair, denial and numbing. The more I delved into the issue, the more alive the reality of our possible annihilation became. The threat to our existence can be a very consuming life and death issue. I read material in waves, needing to digest what I read and regulate my response to the terror inherent in the topic. The readings were both an attempt to educate myself and to assemble a Speakers Bureau Manual to help train psychotherapists to speak knowledgeably to community groups about living in the nuclear age. The reading material made the issues more salient. We also offered workshops, similar to the training I mentioned earlier, that enabled therapists to go through their own process of awakening to living in the nuclear age. The workshops were in California, New York, and Toronto. The responses of people who had previously found it difficult to express their fear and concerns varied from relief in sharing and vocalizing concerns to expressions of deeply held rage, anger, sorrow and mourning. These clinicians were willing to examine how these issues affected their work.

I came out of that year respecting and understanding the need for numbing. I was able and willing to call upon my defenses when necessary so that I wasn't constantly oppressed with the dangers involved in the nuclear threat. I felt respectful of process and timing and the need to meet people where they are. It became easier to hear references to the nuclear issue and respond to it within the clinical hour rather than let it pass unnoticed or unacknowledged. I knew I didn't have all the answers. I didn't have to know what to say to make it better, but I also knew the importance of letting my clients know I heard them and that they were not alone. Their therapy was a place to discuss *all* their fears including their fear for the world. I shared their concern.

At a recent meeting of Psychotherapists for Social Responsibility, Margaret Brenman-Gibson was asked whether or not she thought it relevant and ethical to attune ourselves to the nuclear issue and attend to it as it enters the psychotherapeutic process. She answered that it would be wrong not to; she said that as the fate of humanity was in question, one had the right to make visible the issues and one's values. Just as we work to help clients reflect on the meaning of traumatic events, we must help them explore their thoughts and feelings about the nuclear issue. We must do this in a manner that does not prove traumatic in itself.

CASE VIGNETTES

In my work recently with a fifteen year old and his family, I noticed that the family did not attend to the adolescent's need for assurances and attention related to the nuclear issue. One day in a therapy session, the adolescent yelled, "What difference does it make if I clean up my room or not when the world could blow up any day?" It's possible that this response was merely an example of adolescent rebellion. However, when we stopped and focused on this statement, his parents indicated there had been other references to the nuclear threat that they had not responded to because they didn't know what to say or how to talk about it. The normal sense of helplessness experienced by adolescents seems augmented by the threat of a nuclear holocaust. It's terrifying to grow up in a world that might end at any time. Fears go underground when they are not expressed and acknowledged. Then, they surface in some less healthy manner. It is difficult for adults to respond to children responsibly when their own fears have no place to emerge.

In a recent ongoing therapy group for women with severe physical ailments, a woman wondered if it was appropriate for her to share her fear for the world in the group where people were disclosing personal fears and difficulties about their diseases. With support and encouragement from her therapist, she proceeded to relate her despair for our world, her fear about the ecological imbalance occurring in nature and the indiscriminate manner in which toxic wastes are disposed. As she revealed her concerns and heard people listening, responding and supporting her, she became animated, her skin color changed, her voice deepened and she reported feeling more empowered. It would be naive to think that this woman's experience was only related to her disclosure of her pain for the world. Perhaps it has been difficult for her to share in large groups. Perhaps she is an introverted feeling type who is finding out the possibilities that exist as she reaches out to others. It is important to put this experience in perspective. This is a process. It begins with the therapist listening to individual fears, concerns and beliefs connected to the nuclear peril. It involves cautioning ourselves as therapists to respect the content of material that is presented and remembering to look at the implications of expressing fears and being vulnerable. This can allow us to feel connected.

The dynamics of therapeutic response to the nuclear issue will be different depending on the level of development as well as the diagnosis of each individual client. The metaphorical and actual impact and meaning of the nuclear threat will be experienced differently for each individual. It is necessary to recognize that people may use the nuclear dilemma as a way of avoiding other, more personal, psychodynamic issues. Unable to face their own personal pain, they struggle with their pain for the world. The borderline's fear of annihilation will be enhanced and exaggerated by the nuclear threat. The depressive's attitude of "I don't have a future—Why should I do anything anyway?" will be reflected. The schizophrenic may make an amalgamation of real and inaccurate facts about the bomb. The paranoid personality's belief that some "other" is out to get him or her can certainly be fed by the nuclear threat. The threat of hostility, suspiciousness, and fear that surrounds the escalating arms race can only intensify the paranoid's fear. We would err as clinicians if we did not look to the evocative material of our time and how it affects and intrudes on us. It is more important to take into consideration the real threat of nuclear annihilation, which is universal, and the individual form it takes with each client, as well as the way in which a client integrates and lives with the awareness of the Bomb.

The impact the nuclear issue has in the clinical hour has parallels with racism and sexism. The old argument about the relationship between individual issues of health and community issues of health is called into question. This paper is not focused on this question but it is important to acknowledge the question and to state that for me there is a link between social, political, and humanistic influences and the individual journey in psychotherapy.

Though some of these issues may come up in certain geographical areas more than others, my reading, my practice, and workshops indicate it is representative of our times. Sometimes the issue may come up for examination because there has been a vote in Congress that a client is particularly upset about, or a reference is made to how easily Reagan can reverse a vote in Congress for aid to the Contras. The conversation may begin as chatter. In the past, it may have ended in chatter. At this point I might acknowledge what I heard and ask if the client has any more feelings or thoughts about it. Usually this is met by a statement like, "There really is no place for me to talk about this" or "I try not to think about it too much, it's too upsetting."

Another vignette comes to mind from a supervision group I lead. A therapist reported that his seventeen-year-old female client, Emily, was saying how sad she felt about what was happening in the world. The therapist nodded his head and said nothing. The client proceeded to talk about something else. In supervision, I questioned the therapist about his lack of responsiveness to his client's reference to her pain for the world. He reported that he did not know what to say because he had not examined his own feeling. He indicated that he did not feel like he could help her. The supervision session proceeded with the exploration of the therapist's feeling of inadequacy, numbing, and despair concerning the nuclear issue. Later, he reported that this experience was relieving. Ironically, in his next session with Emily, in an unsolicited moment, Emily mentioned that at fifteen she used to spend hours crying about her belief that she had no future, that the world would be destroyed, that she wouldn't get the chance to grow up and have a career and family of her own. She reported that she would cry daily about it yet never discuss it with anyone. The therapist asked her how she felt about the fate of the earth now. For the next twenty minutes, Emily discussed her concerns for the planet, her own development, and her hopes and fears about the world. The therapist reported that if he had not discussed his own feelings around the nuclear issue, he would have let the reference pass again.

Obviously some movement had occurred for the therapist to be able to pursue the topic more freely. He felt the freedom to encourage her exploration of feelings and thoughts for the world. How often does this occur for all of us in our clinical practice? Why is it so much easier to decide what to do, whether to advise, be supportive, or give opinions to our clients concerning alcoholism, child abuse or fair housing? What needs to happen for an issue to become socially relevant enough for us to feel responsible to touch upon it in the clinical hour? In this supervision group, there were two other instances reported where references were made to the nuclear issue and the fate of the earth. Each therapist chose not to respond because of fear, insufficient information to deal with the nuclear issue, and/or the clinician's own denial.

CASE HISTORIES

Traditional therapy believes itself to be taking a neutral stance toward social issues, and interprets outside concerns as intrapsychic events. But how are we to deal with a concern that is so pervasive in the world? How do we integrate it into our traditional framework without being didactic or proselytizing—i.e., how do we make the discussion therapeutic? I will be sharing two specific case histories to amplify my position. The first case illustrates the possibilities that lie in making connections with an individual's stress and the struggle of living in the nuclear age; the second illustrates a client's pain for the world and her struggle in relating and connecting this pain with her own personal pain.

Sara, thirty, has been in twice-a-week psychotherapy with me for four years. She is the youngest of two siblings from a middle-class family in Cleveland. Her father is a successful corporate lawyer and her mother is an executive for a large computer corporation. The oldest sibling followed in the father's footsteps, went to Harvard, and is also a successful lawyer. Sara is a university graduate currently working for a mental health advocacy agency. Sara is politically savvy, articulate, physically active and living in a committed relationship. She has dealt with such intrapsychic and interpersonal issues as separating from her family and forging an identity of a separate self, breaking away from the professional role her family wanted for her, the disparity between how others see her and her own self-image, her connectedness to her father and her lack of relatedness to her mother, her envy of her sister. Sara is likeable and sincere. She is caring, concerned, and reflective.

There is a strong therapeutic alliance. Initially the transference was an idealized father transference. Although this continues, the primary transference has begun to shift to a mother transference with the emergence of hostile and aggressive feelings. Since the session described below, Sara has become more willing to express negative transference and struggle with her fear of rejection. During a therapeutic hour, Sara may bring in current material or reflect on family-of-origin material and connect the two. She exhibits impressive insight. One of her difficulties is allowing herself to connect with and express the emotional content of the events she is describing. Recently, she has been grappling with issues concerning her career, her choice not to become a lawyer, her desire to go to graduate school to pursue her interest in public policy. However, she has felt stymied.

After struggling with these issues for many months, Sara was able to talk about her sense of being stuck. She summarized many of the issues we had talked about, including her "stuckness." It was at this point that I asked her if there was anything in the outside world that might be affecting her. She sighed, breathed deeply, and slowly began revealing her fears that after five years of graduate school there would be no world left to work in. She felt that time was precious and graduate school seemed like a luxury at a time when our world was in so much turmoil and crisis. She began to sob. My question arose from connecting vague references Sara had made to living in the here and now, and her sensitivity to political, social, and historical events. I knew Sara did not have many outlets to release her feelings and frustrations about many issues.

For the rest of the hour she gave a moving account of the environmental, political and social issues about which she had been feeling despair and concern. The hour was laden with feeling, which is in contrast to her usual style. She was able to cry and felt safe enough to allow her fears to come out. I was deeply moved by the power and depth of the feelings and thoughts she shared. This was visible to Sara and she asked me to share what I had been feeling. I did so. She also asked if I had done my own personal work around the nuclear issue. I told her that I had and that I had similar concerns to her own. I did not feel any hesitation about sharing my own reactions to the issue.

I believe this session was a turning point in Sara's treatment. As I mentioned earlier, the negative transference has emerged more clearly. Sara's willingness to reveal her strongest and deepest feelings and to be seen and accepted in her emotionalism broke through a barrier. It is as if in being seen herself, she was able to see me in my humanness. It was safer to acknowledge my imperfections as she delved into the more difficult places inside herself. Sara more readily brings in fears about the world, her interactions, and her relationships. She is learning to integrate living with her fears and living her life as we all must. This experience strengthened the trust in our relationship and deepened the bond of our connection. This has helped Sara's ability to deepen her process, delve more deeply into herself and take more risks. There is no final resolution yet for Sara. Yet her sense of self and her sense of the world have changed. She is exploring various graduate programs and consumer-oriented jobs. Similarly, there is no final resolution for our own work with the nuclear issue and its integration into our work as clinicians.

Psychodynamically, we can say Sara is dealing with separation anxiety and separation guilt—pre-oedipal issues. Sara fears that if she separates from her family and chooses a different profession she will be annihilated by her family. The nuclear issue and her global concern are a metaphor for her fear, as well as a realistic confrontation with living in the nuclear age. She has found a language to describe her separation anxiety and guilt. This is empowering to her.

For me as a therapist, this experience has raised several important questions. First, could this work have proceeded in the absence of attention to the nuclear issue? I have no doubt that the work with this client would have moved along even if we had not broached the nuclear issue. The sense of annihilation Sara experiences as she approaches conflictual material and whenever she feels that her emotions are getting out of her control have and would have been experienced through other doorways. But her personal sharing about her global concerns was important because she had been unable to talk about these scary feelings with anyone. Sara was able to reveal her dark shadow material, her fears and feelings, with another. She took a risk, she did some reality testing, and she discovered she did not have to hold her dark side to herself.

Second, what has happened within the therapeutic relationship? The discussion of social reality seems to have deepened the therapeutic alliance. Having a safe place to share one's pain is not enough to qualify as empowering for a client. By strengthening the bonds between us, Sara felt safe enough to journey inward, reveal more of herself and take more risks. It is empowering to face and contain fear. It is important to come to terms with what we can do about an issue and come to rest with it.

Third, what is the effect of the therapist sharing her own personal feelings? Certainly, in terms of countertransference, I am aware of both the power and danger inherent in bringing my own material into the clinical hour. It is easy for the therapist to collude with a client by focusing on mutually-accepted important information to the exclusion of other material that could be more fruitful and challenging. And it is easy for the therapist to collude with her client by ignoring material that is dangerous to them both. It is for that reason that I continue to examine vigilantly my own reasons for touching the nuclear issue within the hour. My struggle and work with the countertransference is to differentiate my own issues from those of my clients, to make the necessary distinctions, to respect our differences, and to be as certain as possible that the discussion of social issues serves a therapeutic as opposed to a proselytizing purpose.

Fourth, what is the effect on the therapy when the therapist and client are struggling with the same issue? In the case of the early vignette, sometimes having similar issues clouds the ability of the therapist to see her client's needs. At other times, the therapist needs to be watchful not to intrude his/her own issues with the client. I certainly do not advocate making sure each client I work with deals with his or her nuclear fears. I only hope that we, as clinicians, can begin to hear our client's concerns when they do emerge in the hour.

The second case concerns Harriet, a forty year-old single woman, a university professor and writer, who has been involved in political activities for the last fifteen years. Harriet grew up in an alcoholic family, the oldest of three children. Her father, who owned a Clothing Manufacturing Company, was a workaholic and an alcoholic, not very involved with his family. Her mother, a housewife, was involved with the Church and unavailable emotionally to her children. She returned to work as a school secretary when her children were teenagers. Harriet's family was conservative and apolitical. Harriet's political activism may have been a way to differentiate herself from the conservatism of her family.

Harriet's character is marked by depressive and rigid features. I have seen Harriet for three years in both once-a-week and twice-a-week psychotherapy. During that time, she has dealt with issues of alcoholism including her own dependency, her inability to permit intimacy in relationship, her desire for closeness, her struggles and difficulty with limit-setting and her keen sense of herself as a loser. Harriet suffered many losses as she grew up, including that of a grandmother who was a source of nurturance and acceptance in a sparse emotional environment; a boyfriend from high school and college who was killed in an auto accident; and a professor who was a source of inspiration and guidance to an early death from cancer. These deaths affected Harriet's ability and willingness to reach out to others. It increased her anxiety that intimacy and closeness would endanger the people she most cared for. The political movement gave her a springboard for involvement without risking too much personal interaction. The legacy from her father, an addiction to work, made her successful in her work life. In addition, it prepared her to be valuable to the peace movement, with her unceasing commitment to participate in every action and attend every meeting. Since Harriet experiences her usefulness by her degree of commitment and consistency to a group or cause, it is difficult for her to skip an action or meeting. Work and politics come before self.

Harriet claims she learned early the "alcoholic family" rule: "Don't talk, don't trust, don't feel." At first, our sessions were composed of coping with external events in her life. Often we discussed her political activities, her writing, and her reading. Her presentation was usually highly intellectual and unemotional. Our mutual love of literature became a bridge we could walk upon to strengthen the bond which would eventually allow her to trust, to communicate, and delve into her pain. Her knowledge of my own political activism, through seeing me at various marches, strengthened the trust also. Perhaps my own interest in the fate of the earth permitted me to hear and value what this client was saying. We attune ourselves to hear and value what we consider to be relevant. A clinician's unwillingness, lack of desire, or indifference to the nuclear peril may cause statements referring to the nuclear peril to be overlooked. On the other hand, it is important to recognize the danger inherent in over-identification with issues that both client and therapist think are important. In this case, it was necessary for me to begin to draw metaphors from Harriet's external involvement in the world and apply them to her internal process. It was important for Harriet to find ways to take risks within the structure and framework of her involvement in the peace movement and her identification with the pain and suffering in the world.

Turning points in Harriet's treatment were marked by expressing her feelings to me first through letters and then within the therapeutic hour itself. She reported her pain and suffering for the homeless, for the struggling people of Central America and the abused children of the world. Her denial of her own personal pain and anger was massive at first. Any intervention or interpretation on my part to link the global with the personal was rejected in those first few years. However, certain political events provided a framework for Harriet to experience her acumen, her pain and the respect others had for her perseverance and heart. She began to see her comrades' personal suffering. In an information-gathering trip to another country, Harriet was able to share her fear and vulnerability with the group, and hear their respect for her awareness of her fears and weaknesses. She internalized their encouragement that she face each risk individually and only go as far as she was comfortable.

This was probably one of the first times outside the therapeutic setting that she revealed fears and was respected for it. She discovered the rewards that come from taking risks.

It is still easier for Harriet to express global concerns rather than personal anxieties and fear, but she has become more willing to look to her own painful childhood, her lack of emotional nurturance from either primary parent, and has begun to choose activities that are self-oriented rather than always choosing the collective or the movement. Literature, work, and politics continue to serve as the background and language in which she discovers her self.

In this case, it was important to pay close attention to the counter-transference because of our shared concern for global issues, our activism, our shared language of literature and some early life parallels. I had to be watchful and differentiate Harriet's needs from my own. Interestingly, I had to pay attention to my desire for Harriet to make the link between her global concerns and her personal journey. I needed to be patient and respectful of how her journey unfolded and process my own feelings when she was not able to make the shift from her world pain to her personal pain.

CONCLUSION

On some level, we all are aware of the nuclear threat as well as ecological and environmental threats to our planet. From the therapist's perspective, our own numbing concerning these social realities affects our ability to hear the issues and attend to them when they do enter the clinical hour. It is important that we address our own psychological conflicts concerning the nuclear issue. Being committed to our personal work will enable us to be sensitive to the ways these issues enter the hour. It may enter through dreams, off-the-cuff remarks, chatter, "stuckness," hopelessness, futility, or as pain for the world. The acknowledgement of living under the nuclear shadow, besides being relieving and validating to the client, also provides an entree into other issues our clients may present. The client's relationship to numbing and/or facing nuclear fears provides information about the client's process of denial and openness in general. The importance of this material on an intrapsychic and metaphorical level goes without question. But to err by too quickly interpreting the significance of these external events as intrapsychic, to refuse to acknowledge the reality of the seriousness of the human condition at this point in history, is to fail to validate an important reality we all share.

Jonathan Schell:

Each of us is called on to do something that no member of

any generation before ours has had to do: to assume responsibility for the continuation of our kind—to choose human
survival....For the risk of extinction is not just one more item
on the agenda of issues that face us. Embracing, as it does,
the life and death of every human being on earth and every
future human being, it embraces and transcends all other
issues.[12]

REFERENCES

1. Jonathan Schell, *The Fate of the Earth.* N.Y.: Avon, 1983, p. 148.
2. Judith Lifton, "Psychology: Thinking and Not Thinking about the Unthinkable." In
    Stop Nuclear War! A Handbook. N.Y.: Grove Press, p. 23.
3. Paul Brians, "Americans Learn to Love the Bomb." *The New York Times,* July 17,
    1985, p. A23.
4. John E. Mack, "Psychosocial Effects of the Nuclear Arms Race." *Bulletin of the
    Atomic Scientists,* Vol. 37, No. 4, 1981, pp. 18-23.
5. Sibylle Escalona, "Growing Up with the Threat of Nuclear War: Some Indirect Ef-
    fects on Personality Development." *American Journal of Orthopsychiatry,* Vol. 52,
    No. 4, 1982, pp. 600-607.
6. Benina Berger-Gould, *Growing Up Scared? The Psychological Effect of the Nuclear
    Threat on Children: Strategies for Action* (forthcoming).
7. Scott Hass, Conference: *The Psychological Effect of the Nuclear Threat on Children:
    Strategies for Action.* December 8 and 9, 1984.
8. J. Tatelbaum, *The Courage to Grieve.* N.Y.: Harper and Row, 1984, p. 23.
9. The American Psychiatric Association's Diagnostic and Statistical Manual of Mental
    Disorders (Third Edition), American Psychiatric Association, 1980, p. 236.
10. Schell, p. 152.
11. Margaret Brenman-Gibson. Speech given at a meeting of Psychotherapists for Social
    Responsibility, Berkeley, California, January 12, 1984.
12. Jonathan Schell, quoted in Roger Walsh, *Staying Alive.* Boulder, Colo.: Shambala,
    1984, p. 75.

3

Meditations on Godot: Nuclear Therapy, Death and the Maiden

Paul Olsen, Ph.D.

ESTRAGON: I had a dream.
VLADIMIR: Don't tell me!
ESTRAGON: I dreamt that—
VLADIMIR: DON'T TELL ME!

> Samuel Beckett
> *Waiting for Godot*

The beginning. The dream.

I am sitting quietly in a summer night. Soon there are people milling about with some sort of vague purpose, and without warning airplanes sweep in, roaring and whining low to the ground, igniting everything before us in a napalm sheet of crackling sparks. We crouch together, huddled, in a lean-to shelter made of beams without ceiling or walls. When the planes pass the far horizon begins to glow: dusty pink, dusty rose, mauve, an eerie color I have never seen before. Staring, frightened, mesmerized by that sky, a sick color, nauseating. And then, emerging from the tinted sky, slowly taking shape, hazy then astonishingly clear, a long vertical stalk with a broad round cap, the mushroom. The cap turns until it is a perfect golden circle containing three spokes, the triangle of peace. It stands there against the dusty rose, the symbol of peace, and I wake.

I don't know if I dreamed the dream before or after I heard Jerome Frank relate from *The Words of the Fathers:* "It is not incumbent on you to finish the work; neither are you free to exempt yourself from it."[1] But the dream, the quote, became bonded; and the living thing it formed has in some way formed me. It moved me to a confrontation with nuclear annihilation and the kind of death implied by it. It made me wonder what I was living through as a human being and as a human being who happened to be a psychotherapist.

Now I consider the dream, as some Jungians say, a "big dream," a dream of almost archetypal proportions, not merely a piece of individual intrapsychic life. At first I must have wished it away, interpreting it on a purely personal level, rationalizing it, searching for some day-residue in the faded newspapers of my memory. All dead ends. Then a brief journey into the jungle of pathology: intense rage, a world-destruction fantasy exploding in sleep. Whatever, the dream would not leave my consciousness and I stopped worrying it, picking at it.

A bizarre twist: for a time I preferred to label myself schizoid, a secret schizoid creeping out of one of Harry Guntrip's closets, rather than acknowledging what my dream might have tapped into. Terrifying, I thought, to consider myself damaged beyond all evidence in order to wear Perseus' cap—not merely to hide from monsters but to pretend that they did not exist. It finally made no sense to me that I was carrying around some *utterly unconscious* personal conflict of that size, and I found myself grateful that I was not in psychotherapy at the time—at least the kind of psychotherapy I had been exposed to. My therapist and I might have invented a problem and, thus inventing it, invent a remedy to keep us calm and in control.

What I came to feel, sense, and know was that I had come in touch with something that existed on a number of levels. First, the always-present subterranean knowledge of nuclear annihilation, now turning from possibility to probability, the anxious undercurrent pervading our lives, deadening our hopes, slowly destroying our environment and our connection with it. As if tomorrow will never come, as if today will end before its time. Konrad Lorenz:

> The contemporary infantile striving for instant gratification and the corresponding inability to feel responsible for anything in the more distant future are certainly connected with the fact that at the subconscious root of all decisions lies the anxious question of how long, anyway, the world is going to exist.[2]

More, my awareness that our original and collective dynamics have produced rageful weapons manipulated by primitive rageful people—and the sense that total destruction might be prevented if the threat were faced and felt, if not experienced. "You are either part of the problem, or you are part of the solution."[3] And so am I, and so are my patients, and it can no longer be arguable that we are the caretakers of each others' lives and the lives of our children. No one is exempt.

There is a nuclear war inside us, the revelation of some murderous and ultimately suicidal drift, that has been projected outward not as world-destruction fantasy but as world-destruction reality. The supreme death wish hidden by defensiveness and supported by a repetition-compulsion of historical error: the denial of the war within, its projection onto the "other," and there responded to in the body of the external enemy. We have created a planetary malignancy and we cannot cure it unless we cure ourselves.

Where I am probably most healing is in sessions with my patients, and so it seemed right to work there with the issue of survival. Eventually survival became a place to work *from,* alchemizing it into a powerful response to life. Working on the nuclear threat with patients was not an easy decision although I am not an anonymous therapist and have little commitment to theoretical positions and puzzles. Yet I kept my new involvement with patients mostly secret from my colleagues until one day, at an antinuclear conference, I let it loose. A few other therapists quietly said that they too were working on the issue in sessions. *Mea culpa.* We all felt absolved: we were still therapists, unexcommunicated.

Very important in my decision was, and is, my conviction that the outcome of traditional therapies lacked dimension, passion, connection, blood—the Yiddish *kishkas,* something like guts. To me, former patients seemed left with an excess of narcissism that transformed, behaviorally, to aggrandizement and a cultish individuality paradoxically subservient to the "reality" of authority. "That's reality" always seemed a catchphrase, as if it explained, interpreted, and justified almost everything without its intrinsic helplessness being grasped. This thought, this possibility, appeared absolutely alien: "Philosophers have only *interpreted* the world in various ways; the point is to *change* it."[4] (For "philosopher" read "psychotherapist"—the patient being the philosopher's disciple.)

Perhaps interpersonal relationships fared better, but I rarely if ever perceived a deeper in-touchness with larger possibilities, a recognition that we are *all* connected in this evolutionary maelstrom, not just attached to a lover, spouse, friend, ethnic or religious group. Trigant Burrow elaborated this perception many years ago in his attempt to incorporate social meaning into psychotherapy:

...*my* opinion and *my* wish are, of course, supreme. But John and Mary are also social beings and equally supreme in their affectively encapsulated "I" personae. They and everyone else are as "right" in their private absolutism and autocracy as I am in mine. Lacking the motivation or behavior that is physiologically continuous, having substituted the premise that the organism's motivation rests upon a basis that is private and dichotomous, our reactions can only be private and dichotomous also. We may only *deal with* one another; we may not be *united as* one another. If there is conviviality and accord, it is...because momentarily the self-interest of each of us happens to correspond in its outward form.[5]

The "successful" patient or analysand tended to stay in his or her own backyard (the area might have expanded somewhat), periodically checking the soundness of the fence and keeping rigid guard at the gate. This was also true of the groups in which I had participated, where each member had experienced roughly a decade of individual psychotherapy—and we were all rehashing the same old "material" as if we had never been in therapy at all. Simply moving around the backyard covering inches of familiar terrain, perhaps plucking a weed—addicted, I think, to our intrapsychic wounds. There were many vibrant wishes expressed but no one ever acted on them; no one ever wanted passionately to leave the snug place we knew so well. (Or had we once experienced something then driven it away? Like feeling the power and spirit of Beethoven, then "forgetting" them an hour after the concert.) And we were all burdened, seeming not to know that the world was drifting toward terminal illness and that we were part of that world, that something was keeping us invalid, helpless, and perplexingly oppressed, wandering through our lives "lightly chlorophormed."[6]

Vicki Lee writes:

Perhaps our most subtle means of unconscious oppression lies in supporting our clients' choices to "marry while Rome burns"—to focus great energy on resolving exquisitely personal issues and no energy upon political change. Assisting patients to foster self-esteem in their 5-year-old while ignoring the threat to the actual survival of that child and her planet is garden variety clinical practice; from a certain painful vantage point it is suicidal.[7]

Can the introduction of, or response to, nuclear concerns in psychotherapy produce a deeper sense of potency and meaning in our patients? I have little doubt of it. Entering a context in which great action is required lends perspective to our individual conflicts; we become the microcosm of the larger issue; we can understand that since we are responsible for making the world as it is, we can also work to change it. That *we* are *it,* we do not stand aside, above, or out of it. Some freedom from oppressive self-interest, rooted in indifference to the globality that nurtures us, is then possible, and without that freedom we all remain victims of what *they* are doing to *us,* we cling more desperately to our little backyards.

Quite simply, and unarguably if we attend even cursorily to what has become of our environment, the planet will no longer suffer the delusion that we are larger than it or that we are not a living, active part of it. And by planet I mean not only people, but animals, birds, insects, mountains, rivers, oceans, air—all of it. They will not permit us to indulge our false separations, our apartness; every day they show us what we have done to them. Their ruin must bring our own. Unamuno said it well, that "if the individual survives through his instinct for self-preservation, society owes its being and its continuance to the instinct for perpetuation in the individual. And, from this instinct, or rather from society, springs reason."[8]

We exist in a context, and it is less an issue to badger patients with fears of Armaggedon than it is to call attention to the context, to provide it if necessary, to help put things where they belong. For example: a patient was plagued by a profound spider phobia. When I asked her to close her eyes and visualize a spider, it hung huge and ominous in dark space. Gradually we constructed a river bank, trees, bushes, flowers, grass—until the spider sat in a web strung between two branches, small in proportion to its environment, no longer looming in a space without referents or context.

Life, sharply focused, lies just beneath fears of nuclear annihilation. Inescapably in our time—yet perhaps it is the legacy of our species—we must confront and work through the threat of doom in order to get to the life. Like the process of Joanna Macy's rituals and exercises,[9] we can tunnel through helplessness and despair out into a spontaneous feeling of aliveness and empowerment. Patients, as well as therapists, frequently begin to sense their interconnectedness and their relation to the larger world that *literally* sustains them; and that we all have the power to destroy and to create.

There is no *Bomb.* The *Bomb* is a deification, a phobic abstraction looming in a space without context. But there are nuclear weapons conceived and controlled by human beings. And human beings can dismantle them and reduce them to piles of junk. If I can see how I have helped build these weapons, if I involve myself with them, with the shared consciousness that forged them, with the life their absence implies, I can understand how to disintegrate them. I must become aware that my rage and alienation have built these weapons just as, on only an *apparently* different level, my rage may drive away my lover. It is the same rage and I must come to terms with it in order to save my life; and, once saved, I earn the luxury to enhance it.

A recent book outlines some 250 identifiable modalities of psychotherapy.[10] Most cannot be wholly integrated although one modality might incorporate various techniques from another. But issues of nuclear annihilation versus planetary life should be amenable to introduction into any of these "schools"; yet if by their very nature they cannot endure or support this incorporation, then they cannot be called therapeutic in any species-connected way. Psychotherapy then clings to the most traditional of medical models: lancing a boil or excising an appendix with no concern for the development of an awareness of the world in which the patient lives and for whose health and preservation she or he is responsible. No awareness of "the shared disorder of the community *as it operate[s] within their own organisms.*"[11] Nor, for that matter, of the potentiality of a shared *order.* Nothing happens except that we may "feel better" through cosmetic surgery or become more "functional" in our encapsulation.

Of course the question of values will arise here since we have been trained, even warned, to exclude them from the treatment situation. But any one of the 250 modalities of psychotherapy is a value system, collective and personal, into which the *patient is introduced.* That process has received an imprimatur because most of these schools protest their "scientific" objectivity (or attempts at it) and fervidly deny their quasi-religious aspects—i.e., their value-laden infrastructures. They could not stand in such *general* opposition to each other, could not squabble so unremittingly, if their territories were not charged by values and beliefs. Holy wars.

It might be inappropriate to inform a patient of my racism, of the "truth" of my true religion, of my rabid distaste for a particular person. But the discussion of our survival as a species cannot remotely be construed as a personal value unless we have deeply lost touch: Alfreda S. Galt explicating Trigant Burrow: "the 'solidarity of the species' is the *primary* motivating force for human behavior—and the overlying self-orientation, extending throughout interpersonal and intergroup relations, is secondary."[12]

No defense of this species-value appears necessary to me. Directly to the point is the report of an encounter with Margaret Brenman Gibson, who "was asked whether or not she thought it relevant and ethical to bring the nuclear issue into the psychotherapeutic process. She replied that it would be wrong not to, remarking that as the fate of humanity was in question, one had the right to make visible the issues and one's own values."[13] In order to make such a statement, one must of course possess the value.

ESTRAGON: The best thing would be to kill me,
                 like the other.
VLADIMIR: What other?...What other?
ESTRAGON: Like billions of others.

                . . . .
VLADIMIR: It's evening, Sir, it's evening,
                 night is drawing nigh....I have
                 lived through this long day and I
                 can assure you it is very near the
                 end of its repertory.

I make the assumption that the major requirement of any therapeutic
process is that the people in the consulting room be alive. This assumption is not so obvious; we do not give it enough weight. When patients
are late for sessions we rarely, if ever, wonder if they are dead—unless
they are suicidal. Like a habit or an addiction we usually slide into an interpretation that focuses on acting-out of some sort, but we never
wonder if the person is dead. Death is infrequently addressed at all; if it
occurs to us, we look to countertransference for an answer, and of
course we will find one. The closest we come is when a patient is literally
dying; symbolically, when a patient wishes to leave therapy and we allot
an amount of time during which to discuss the termination—trying to
deal with that analogue of dying, a poor one though it may be. The event
of "premature" termination is traditionally shorthanded as "losing" the
patient; the verb denotes the chief mourner.

When a patient develops a potentially terminal illness we participate in
an event that, possibilities of empathy aside, only one of us is truly experiencing. We, therapists, may try to participate more fully, but like as
not we will harness all our available defenses and activate those of our
patient. (That is not to say that we are not feeling what we are able to
feel.) The event is as a rule rarely an open, free encounter in which *each*
person permits full emotional expression; we may even discourage it. The
stance emerges from a conviction that illness and impending death require a great deal of defending, including denial, if one is to go on living
while one eye stares at the grave. And the parallel to nuclear holocaust is
clear: a global extension of a personal terror, both eliciting defensive
coping.

We deny the impact of the terminal situation, or assume a
"therapeutic" posture, or grow covertly enraged and depressed because
our patient (or the media) has brought death into our lives and attacked
us with it. "[R]epression," Ernest Becker said, "takes care of the complex symbol of death for most people," but "underneath the most bland

exterior lurks the universal anxiety, the 'worm at the core' ''[14]—the fear of death and of our connection to it.

To repress this anxiety, to deny that death is a crucial, incontrovertible aspect of the process of living, is to act it out aggressively, to impound it suicidally, or to project it as an act or set of attitudes aimed at destroying us. (We must maintain physical strength to prevent a heart attack; we must maintain military strength to prevent a Soviet attack.) The veiled fear of death lies at the root of nuclear denial, and so we are loath to introduce the nuclear disaster into sessions or even to confront it in its own terms. When I once remarked to a colleague that I had never seen despair expressed more profoundly than in response to this issue, he replied: "There's more to it than just that." Maybe. Maybe not.

The point is that we dance around the nuclear nightmare as we dance around a physically intact patient's fear of death by inquiring into depression, morbidity, internalized anger, some other personal pathology. But the facile classical choreography does not mesh with the atonality. We simply cannot deal with the fear itself—a universally shared fear—as if it is not part of life, as if death is not by definition woven into the very fabric of life, as if it is an unexpected event, a nuclear detonation preceded by a brief siren wail of painful comprehension.

What is inescapable in our nuclear environment, the tons of TNT allocated to *each* human being in a superpower nation, is that we are all living in a potentially terminal situation regardless of age or state of health. In microcosm, patient and therapist are sitting together in a terminal situation. If I as therapist work with my patient as though she or he is suffering from morbid ideas for which the terminal situation is solely symbolic of underlying psychodynamics, then I am launching a collusion—a collusion that will rigidify defenses in both of us and encourage a false and dangerous optimism. I will be turning my patient and myself away from a profound reality—the real threat of extinction and the real possibility of effective action—by manipulating him or her into feeling more "comfortable" with negative personal dynamics while my own security will be established through my theoretical and technical acumen.

There is irony here. And enormity. (Recall my strange "comfort" in diagnosing myself schizoid in preference to admitting that I might have tapped into a very shattering reality.) I will be colluding in a charade, not unconscious but lacking consciousness, like the lunatic evacuation plans that will work smoothly if the Soviet Union informs us a week in advance of its intent to launch a surprise nuclear attack, like government spokesman T.K. Jones's assurance that nuclear war can be survived by digging a hole and waiting it out: "If there are enough shovels to go around, everybody's going to make it."[15] A collusion that, piled upon countless other collusions, may well contribute not only to the destruction of the two of us in the room, but to the destruction of the planet.

Again, the therapeutic microcosm: a colleague recently demanded that a patient, after blandly reporting a series of automobile skids, put chains on his tires since every morning he drove on icy suburban roads past a busy school crossing. Demanded it in order to protect his patient's life as well as the lives of the children and other drivers. He remarked that "by the time we got through working with the acting-out in the usual way it would have been spring and we'd be holding sessions in the funeral parlor. I didn't think it could wait that long."

Explaining dangerous or upsetting external events by pulling them into a personal psychodynamic framework ("...outside myself there is a world," William Carlos Williams reminds us) is in part a result of Freud's anger, bitterness, and feelings of helplessness. Carl E. Schorske recounts Freud's early inability to achieve academic status primarily because he was a Jew in Catholic Vienna. Focusing internally on his relationship to his father and "to lay his father's ghost Freud had either, like Hamlet, to affirm the primacy of politics by removing what was rotten in the state of Denmark (a civic task) or to neutralize politics by reducing it to psychological categories (an intellectual task)."[16] Thus, in analyzing his dreams with an emphasis upon his dead father as powerful king-inhibitor, "psychoanalysis overcomes history. Politics is neutralized by a counterpolitical psychology."[17]

By this sleight of mind Freud rendered his social plight more manageable through a sense of intellectual mastery, but it did not result in academic advancement. He obtained it instead "at a high moral cost. For, against his conscience. Freud had recourse to what was known in Austria as 'protection'—the help of socially influential individuals to receive personal preferment."[18] An analysis of unconscious death wishes, the intellectual "mastery" of them, would not have saved the lives of the driver-patient or the schoolchildren; the reduction of nuclear fears to personal psychodynamics will not alter political consciousness toward the abolition of weapons and the prevention of annihilation. It is probably suicidal to help patients "overcome history" by analyzing away its legacy and ramifications when they must confront the world of which they are an active part. And the nuclear threat will not vanish through "protection." We might, however, take a dual approach, connecting the intrapsychic life to the facts of the outside world since our internal turmoil has brought us to the edge of global chaos. But reductionism alone cannot alleviate any external situation especially when the state of Denmark smells to high heaven.

Returning to images of death. One of my patients developed a cancer and I listened very carefully to what she said, to her sequence of feelings and thoughts, kept track of her actions. At first she was depressed, panicky, felt a fragmentation of her body image and image of self, almost overwhelmed by despair and helplessness, especially helplessness. I said very little except when she wanted me to say something. I watched her slowly work through her feelings, see her illness as a process, learn about it, and begin to take charge. Her insistence on involvement with her illness—moving from a passive helpless victim to an active participant—initially maddened her physicians, until they responded fully, even with a trace of love. She healed herself emotionally if not physically—but perhaps that too. The process was reminiscent of a statement by Joanna Macy: "Despair and empowerment work helps us to increase our awareness...without feeling overwhelmed by... dread, grief, anger and [a] sense of powerlessness..."[19] And, consistently, it closely followed the forward movement of nuclear workshops that focus primarily on the expression of emotion: a movement through helplessness, rage, and despair to a position of increased balance and consciousness. It all takes time and commitment: we drift so easily back to passivity, numbness, and denial.

The denial of death is catastrophic; it does not lead to a fuller sense of life, but to the marketplace of the myriad narcotics we have invented to dull an almost indefinable pain—or a pain we dare not identify. Psychotherapy, too, can become an opiate: false mastery; planetary death an abstraction; sublime unconcern; a myopic vision of social and historical imperatives. On balance, the importance of unrepressing the "worm at the core" is the budding awareness of a process that must be embraced if the whole of our lives is to be experienced. I must deal with my death if my life is not to be terminal—and I may exit peacefully in my sleep or in hair-tearing agony or by my own hand if I cannot abide the pain and the indignity. But I claim my death as I claim my life, and I will not be robbed of it. I will not allow myself passively to be murdered on a sacrificial altar of political manipulation and madness masquerading as reason. To bring this passivity to our sessions is as destructive as bringing it to any situation in which we make contact with a living creature.

It is a great temptation to wonder if, after all, Freud was correct in one of his widely refuted ideas: that a death instinct may reside deeply in the genes of our species, "a wish to dissolve, annihilate *oneself,* while the destructive-instinct...implies a wish to kill *others.*"[20] I begin to believe Freud here but I think these two "instincts" are not so discrete: the absence of wholesale opposition to the threat of extinction suggests that the wish to kill others grows indistinguishable from the wish to annihilate oneself. There is still serious talk of winning a nuclear war, of surviving a nuclear war, of limited nuclear war-fighting, despite an enormous amount of perhaps incontrovertible data to the contrary. That is the aggressive facade that masks our craving for self-annihilation, except that if the facade is maintained and strengthened both desires are welded into a seamless destructive whole. As Tom Lehrer would have it, "We will all go together when we go."[21]

If no such instincts exist, all well and good; even so, some hope emerges from the observation that in humans instincts are generally open-ended and are thus amenable to directional change. On the other hand we may simply be suicidal. Never has a species conspired to make its entire environment insupportable; never has a species acquiesced so passively and yet so unremittingly to its own terminal course.

Margaret Brenman Gibson cannot be gainsaid: it is wrong not to let the condition be known, and wrong not to infuse a dangerously destructive situation with the values of survival and life. And if my patients and I cannot share this together, who then are we? *What* are we? And what odd game is being played out in that room?

VLADIMIR:	Well? What do we do?
ESTRAGON:	Don't let's do anything. It's safer.
VLADIMIR:	Let's wait and see what he says.
ESTRAGON:	Who?
VLADIMIR:	Godot.

While the number of psychotherapists involved with the nuclear disaster is growing (though hardly a majority), I have nevertheless wondered why so many of us do not, will not, or cannot address this issue, and of course the reasons are multileveled and multidetermined. Aside from the anxiety that cuts across all professional and social strata, with therapists there is again the idea that only personal I-oriented "material" is appropriate in treatment and that this material should emerge primarily from the patient—a position, perhaps ossified, held even by therapists who are anti-nuclear activists away from their sessions. (Yet there are such typical stories as this, from a colleague: "My analyst keeps hammering at me that I want my father's penis. I don't know where he's getting it from because it sure as hell isn't coming from me.") Some therapists appear to know nothing at all about the issue, ostensibly uninterested, a kind of hair-raising "It-has-nothing-to-do-with-me" attitude. And it is difficult not to construe this attitude as defensive. One recalls that in 1938 Ernest Jones had practically to pry Freud out of Vienna while the streets bulged with Nazis who had already ransacked the Freud household, intimidated Anna, and would in a very short time be shipping Jews to Dachau.[22] The Gestapo stood physically in his home and still he was defending. How much easier it is to defend against a nuclear Dachau when missiles are inundated by rhetoric and the destruction of Hiroshima and Nagasaki occurred 40 years ago, "over there," and to an alien race of people that is now almost the economic master of the world.

And some argue the familiar arguments: deterrence, bargaining from strength, the knavery of the Soviets, the defense of freedom—ad infinitum.

I believe that a broader issue exists, or at least a more pervasive one, that centers on the implications of professionalism in American culture, and the implications run deep since professionalism transubstantiates to identity. I am what I do. Professionalism is a container for pride, status, economic clout, reflected self, a high "life-style" (no working person struggling financially could conceivably have coined the term).[23] Psychotherapists are victims of a further superiority: they *know* more than other people, they are diviners of human behavior and motivation, they not only possess special technical knowledge—as do physicists and lawyers—but they also *know why* these professionals chose their dynamically determined specialties. And the power of the mind takes primacy over experience (I can still be lectured on aggression even though I served in the army in Korea). Further, in many cases therapists have absorbed the traditional functions of clergy and family.

Power indeed, and of a proportion not readily or easily relinquished. Conversely, it is clung to tenaciously and it does not stimulate risk-taking—particularly among psychotherapists whose core beliefs and theoretical understanding may be turned inside-out. Just one example: if once I wanted to "save the world," I was grandiose, perhaps paranoid; but now, with 50,000 warheads primed, the "Star Wars" delusion promulgated by the present Administration, the environment dangerously toxic, animal species vanishing daily—who will save the world if I do not? The experts? Because they are the professionals?

The very training of psychotherapists goes against it all, whether medical or non-medical. We are immersed in the training and its incumbent attitudes directly we enter the graduate world, with little or no life experience to provide a context for the occult nature of what we are to learn. (Indeed, there seems a growing trend away from accepting older students in favor of ever-brighter youngsters with astronomical GRE scores, a trend reminiscent of Jesuits of bygone days who said—in paraphrase—"Give me the child as young as you can and he will belong to us forever.") The thrust toward specialization begins instantaneously. I remember how annoyed and disgruntled my classmates were when, by an old university rule, we were required to take a number of credits outside the psychology program. What could Faulkner teach us about human beings? Or Woolf, Dostoevsky, Nietzsche, Jane Austen, Marx, even Oscar Lewis?

On our one-track journey toward expertise we learn about symptoms, character disorders, psychoses, medication, psychopathy and sociopathy, but literally nothing about the emotional illnesses bred by a depleted, aggressive, overly-competitive society; instead we are asked to join it. And we rarely dirty our hands with the poor; modern "talk" therapy, with its analytic underpinnings was, after all, conceived and born in the ambulatory wards of the middle and upper classes. So there is a pro-establishment bias built into the way we look at our patients (Ronald Laing rebelled and had his disciples, but by American time standards that was a century ago). We place unbearable emphasis on family history, parental influence, intrapsychic dynamics, invisible structures, but never, in any meaningful way, on what the social structure does to us. Because we cannot; that is the seedbed of our professionalism and that is where our identities and incomes can be terminated. Stress kills, but the trend is to accept it or drug it away, even to use it as a motivator. We have never been taught prevention or urged to cure the roots of the damage; so that our psychotherapy is too often a mop-up operation, a post-combat detail cleaning up the wounded. Optimally we say that structural change has occurred. The healthy analysand marches back into the maw, gets devastated all over again, and we sift through our therapeutic ''errors'' without once asking: ''What the hell are they doing to us out there? What am I doing to contribute to this?''

Angry. Perhaps too passionate.

Passion drives the mind.

And so into my sessions I introduce the issue of survival, of life waiting within the nuclear presence—but not with all patients, though I can't articulate the reasons why I demur. And I unfailingly respond to it when it appears spontaneously in associations, worries, dreams, and imagery. I have no formula, no paradigms; other therapists might. I will inquire into a posture that defends against a larger idea, and often I will interpret the seeming lack of concern, the indifference to involvement, the self-removal from the web of life. To me, encapsulation is deadening in any person I try to contact. And I have not yet seen any negative effects in the therapeutic process; to the contrary, the opening of encapsulation has been powerfully positive. Meaning emerges—meaning, that elusive grail—and becomes process, and it derives in large part from attending seriously to the world and one's connection to it, not merely from personal gratification, goal-directed activity, and feeling good. There is pain in it, and beauty in it—and that is finally what our psychotherapies have lacked. An aesthetic, a sense of creative force in working with the materials of our environment.

In this spirit I will occasionally introduce the nuclear issue to a pregnant patient (I have never, anyway, regarded pregnancy as a sacred therapeutic avoidance). I take this seriously because a new child is not only a potential contribution to individual lives, but because a fresh life is being brought in to join and participate in a species-movement that needs every bit of solidity and connection to life it can get. My own children are aware of the threat that surrounds them, and are better off to have avoided any delusional efforts at protectiveness I might have made; they witness my activity and from there must spring their hope and potency. So my patient and I may talk of responsibility—and go on from there.

Otherwise it spins out as it will, spontaneously for the most part. I have nuclear literature in my office; an award I received for nuclear-education work hangs on a wall. A poster, a button. My patients may know of conferences and workshops I have helped organize; they may have read an article of mine. At any rate they are aware of it; it is always there in the room in one form or another. My opinions and feelings are always visible. It is a topic I cannot be cagey about.

The times beg for a different kind of psychotherapy—and we must work to unfold it—as they beg for a different kind of politics, spirit, and necessity. The old way is no longer adequate, and it is just possible that it never was. It lulls us into the illusion that nothing is different and that all is well, when in fact very little is well. *Maya,* it is called in India: illusion and the creation of illusion.

> Until we can extend our psychotherapy...we will no doubt continue our habit of giving highly destructive weapons to infantile leaders, who may yet use them to solve their personal problems and thereby end both our psychohistory and our psychotherapy together in one big bang.[24]

ESTRAGON: You dreamt it....Are you sure
             it wasn't him?
VLADIMIR: Who?
ESTRAGON: Godot.

I go to bed and close my eyes and Dylan Thomas tells me not to go gently into that dark night.

I go to my love who puts her arms around me and reassures all the pieces of my being.

I go to fragments of "Death and the Maiden," a poem by Matthias Claudius, who died at the age of 20, a poem that gave Schubert a beautiful song and a monumental string quartet.

"*Vorüber, ach vorüber,*" the girl cries out. "Go away, let me *be.* Dear God, how can you cut me down before I've even flowered? I beg you. I beg you don't touch me."[25]

The maiden. The earth, the planet, all that holds me.

I go to my sleep and to a dream.

> I am sitting on a broken stone in a field of endless rubble. Crumbled brick, shards of glass, chunks of scarred metal twisted into ugly shapes. The sky is gray with deeper gray

48

patches and all around is a smell of burned fish. I am covered
with a coat of ash that clings to me like paste. I am exhausted,
almost mindless, as if I have not slept or eaten for days. I
should get up and go away but I can't get up and anyway
there is no place to go. I know that because as far as my eyes
can see, everything is the same expanse of wreckage, of
nothing, and a mist is crawling in from the horizon.

To my right a man appears, or maybe he has been there all
the while. There is nothing at all remarkable about his size or
weight or face. He has eyes like my own. He is dressed in a
trim gray suit, dark red tie, black leather gloves, his shoes
gleam. He is carrying what looks like a briefcase and a umbrella rolled so tightly it resembles a cane, a walking stick.

He tilts his face upward and flares his nostrils at the air,
trying, it seems, to place the smell. It offends him like a person he finds annoying and must stand above. His face is dis-
dainful and, when he finally looks my way, contemptuous.
He stands in the rubble like a statue, cut stone in gray and
black, a small sop to life in the color of his tie. Out there,
beyond him, the mist is spreading.

I raise my arm and describe an arc parallel to the ground, a
long arc from right to left, and try to say *Look.* The word
doesn't come but I can feel it framed on my lips and tongue.
He answers quickly, loudly, his voice surrounding me: *Irrelevant,* he booms. I cock my head and perhaps he thinks I
didn't hear him. *Irrelevant,* he says again.

Then he turns smartly and begins to move off, and some
sort of matter rises from the broken ground and moves slowly
up his legs. The gleaming shoes are gone, his clothes are soo-
ty. His shoulders collapse a little, the matter rises up his body,
and with intense determination he straightens his posture, un-
furls his umbrella, and spreads it above him. Then walks
slowly away and merges with the mist.

REFERENCES

1. Jerome Frank, *Preparing for Nuclear War: The Psychological Effects.* N.Y.: Physicians for Social Responsibility, 1982, p. 75. Proceedings of a symposium held in New
York City, February 13, 1982.
2. Konrad Lorenz, *Civilized Man's Eight Deadly Sins.* N.Y.: Harcourt Brace
Jovanovich, 1974, pp. 99-100.
3. Douglas Marshall, *The Cape Codder,* January 25, 1985, p. 5
4. Karl Marx, "Theses on Feuerbach." In *The Portable Karl Marx,* edited by Eugene
Kamenka, N.Y.: Viking Penguin, 1983, p. 158.
5. Trigant Burrow, *Science and Man's Behavior.* N.Y.: Philosophical Library, 1953, pp.
242-243.

6. Saul Bellow, *To Jerusalem and Back: A Personal Account.* N.Y.: Harper and Row, 1977, p. 111.

7. Vicki Lee, "International Psychotherapists for Peace: A Vision." *Transactional Analysis Journal,* Vol. 14, No. 4, October, 1984, p. 237.

8. Miguel de Unamuno, *The Tragic Sense of Life in Men and Nations.* Princeton, N.J.: Princeton University Press, 1972, p. 29.

9. Joanna Rogers Macy, *Despair and Personal Power in the Nuclear Age.* Philadelphia: New Society Publishers, 1983.

10. Richie Herink, ed., *The Psychotherapy Handbook.* N.Y.: New American Library (Meridian), 1980.

11. Alfreda S. Galt, "Trigant Burrow and the Phylobiological Perspective." *Somatics,* Autumn/Winter 1984-85, p. 57.

12. Ibid.

13. Ellen Becker, "The Nuclear Issue in the Therapeutic Process." *Therapy Now,* Vol. 1, No. 2, 1984, p. 13.

14. Ernest Becker, *The Denial of Death.* N.Y.: The Free Press, 1973, pp. 20-21.

15. Robert Scheer, *With Enough Shovels: Reagan, Bush & Nuclear War.* N.Y.: Random House, 1982, p. 18.

16. Carl E. Schorske, *Fin-de-Siècle Vienna.* N.Y.: Knopf, 1980, p. 186.

17. Ibid., p. 197.

18. Ibid., p. 203.

19. Joanna Rogers Macy, *Despair and Personal Power in the Nuclear Age,* p. 1 of unpaginated Introduction.

20. Charles Rycroft, *A Critical Dictionary of Psychoanalysis.* N.Y.: Basic Books, 1968, p. 27.

21. Tom Lehrer, *Too Many Songs by Tom Lehrer.* N.Y.: Pantheon, 1981, p. 81.

22. Russell Jacoby, *The Repression of Psychoanalysis.* N.Y.: Basic Books, 1983.

23. Dobbie Sanders, a skilled Black worker: "...I just got tired of the whole thing and quit work. I enrolled in the L.L. Cooke School of Electronics in Chicago....But I came on back to Fairfield [Alabama]....So when I got back here, the head of the school in Chicago called the people at U.S. Steel and told them what I could do. But they said they wasn't hiring no colored electricians. They still made me do electrical work sometimes, but they just didn't pay me for it." Groesbeck Parham & Gwen Robinson, "If I Could Go Back." In Marc S. Miller, ed., *Working Lives.* N.Y.: Pantheon, 1980, p. 44.

24. Lloyd deMause, "Psychohistory and Psychotherapy." *History of Childhood Quarterly: The Journal of Psychohistory,* Vol. 2, No. 3, 1975, p. 414.

25. Deepest thanks to Dr. Deborah Rinzler whose inherent artistic sense and intuition restored my translator's imagination and freedom. I was somewhat stuck by Claudius's poem, especially by his figure for death, *Knochenman,* literally "bone-man"—and that would not do. Nor was "skeleton" a happier substitute. The libretto translation of *Knochenman* is the certainly unacceptable "scythe-man," and nowhere can I find *knoch* or *knochen* translated as "scythe." But the cutting image captured me and held the intended power of the poem.

    I am aware of the sexual implications of the lines and perhaps I have even strengthened them; the rape of the young girl is an apt analogue to the rape of the earth before it has come full flower—which for some reason, utterly mysterious to me, reminds me of that most beautiful of all titles, Proust's *A l'Ombre des jeunes filles en fleur.*

    The gist of it all, I think, resides in Pablo Neruda's lines: *Y las lenguas del hombre se juntaron/en la primera ira, antes del canto.* (And the tongues of men came together/ first in rage, before there was song.)

4

A Proposal for a Nuclear Tensions Monitoring Center

Lloyd deMause

Most discussions of nuclear war agree upon one point: the total irrationality of the present nuclear buildup. Since we now know that the explosion of less than one percent of our present nuclear stockpile could bring about a nuclear winter and end all sentient life on earth, our continuing to multiply the overkill ratio seems beyond the powers of any psychology to explain. As George Kennan has put it, "we have gone on piling weapon upon weapon, missile upon missile...like men in a dream [until] today we and the Russians [have attained] levels of redundancy such as to defy rational understanding."[1]

Yet the answer to the question "Why do we continue to build more nuclear weapons" is, I have come to believe, a simple one: "Because we want to have a nuclear war." Few have argued such a motivation. The observation that conscious fears are often fueled by unconscious wishes is a familiar one for psychotherapists, who are used to hearing their patients complain about situations which they themselves have worked hard to bring about. Even so, the notion that we are continuing to build nuclear weapons because we actually want to use them seems hard to accept.

The reasons *why* we want to have wars, including a nuclear war, are—like the reasons why individuals engage in other kinds of self-destructive acts—more complex, and involve an understanding of the deepest layers of the unconscious mind. The motives behind past wars have been the subject of study for two decades by research associates at The Institute for Psychohistory. These investigations have focused on the fantasy content expressed in the words and images used by national leaders and the media *prior* to wars. We have been surprised to find consistent patterns of group-fantasies which nations share and use as trial actions in the process of finding an enemy and beginning a war. From the fantasy analysis of tens of thousands of public documents such as presidential speeches, press conferences, media imagery and political cartoons, researchers have found that wars have always been preceded by a period during which there is a buildup of internal psychological tensions which do not originate in the international sphere at all. The group-fantasies which are circulated in the public dialogue during this buildup of tensions include growing guilt over sinfulness, despair about ever achieving happiness, increasing rage and fears of ego collapse, and, finally, powerful wishes to sacrifice youth as representatives of forbidden sexuality and rebelliousness. In analyses of periods prior to World War I, World War II, the Korean War, the Vietnam War and the present period under the Reagan Administration,[2] investigators have discovered that in nations, as in individuals, if one listens to the unconscious messages embedded in the public dialogue, one finds that people usually tell you in advance what they are about to act out.

This is not new to the psychotherapist. When a patient comes in several times and reports dreams all of which involve some harm coming to his or her spouse, the therapist begins to question whether a wish to harm the spouse might not be about to be acted upon. Similarly, when nations begin to "dream" in unison of sacrificing children and harming young people, even though those images are hidden beneath a set of defenses which rationalize their presence, there is also reason to believe the nation is about to act upon these wishes. Our study of the past has demonstrated that these images appear regularly before wars and at no other times. We have found them not only lawful, but predictable. Once one learns how to decode the national dream images by which hidden wishes are communicated, there is less reason to be surprised by overt hostilities when they do occur.

While there is not space here in which to review the large literature on group-fantasies which precede wars,[3] I do want to provide a brief summary of some of the most salient conclusions of psychohistorical research. These conclusions form a coherent theory of war which is truly psychogenic, as opposed to the economic theories of war which are most common today.[4]

THE PSYCHOGENIC THEORY OF WAR

1. *War is a wish,* not a "response" or a "mistake," involving a period of regression which is similar to the regressions ex-

perienced by individuals during psychotic episodes.[5]

2. *This group regression is signaled by violent group-fantasies* which reflect growing rage and fears of national collapse, desires for national rebirth through violence and fantasies of cleansing of sinfulness.

3. *The regression occurs after periods of prosperity and progress,* when the punitive superego is called forth by a nation's success and by unaccustomed personal freedoms.

4. *War is a delusional solution to these psychotic anxieties,* an ego-reintegrating clarification of the confusions and free-floating paranoid feelings of the previous period, so that finding an "enemy" is at first felt to be a release of tension.

5. *War involves a grandiose sexualization of inner conflict,* accompanied by group-fantasies of rape and orgasmic violence, projected into an appropriate "enemy" who has agreed to participate in a period of mutual sacrifice.

6. *Killing an "enemy" represents killing inner desires* and is therefore a victory for "good"—the punitive superego—over "evil"—the dangerous id.

7. *War is a sacrificial ritual* in which the blood of soldiers is drained away to cleanse the nation and remove its sinfulness and make it good again.

If the general dimensions of this psychogenic theory of war have any validity, it follows that the most effective help which the mental health profession can provide for a world which is preparing for a suicidal nuclear war is to *make the unconscious conscious,* just as they have been trained to do in the case of individuals. Since an unconscious wish derives its power to be acted upon through its state of repression, the group-fantasy of having a cleansing nuclear war can only be prevented from being acted out by continuous interpretations of both the wish and its myriad defense systems. Therefore, I would like to propose that psychotherapists, psychiatrists, psychohistorians, political psychologists and other specialists who might be trained in the analysis of unconscious mental life establish a Nuclear Tensions Monitoring Center whose purpose would be to describe, measure and publicize increases in violent group-fantasies in each of the nuclear nations and to give continuous psychological help in decreasing nuclear tensions.[6]

Although such a Monitoring Center would be difficult to establish and sustain, given the history of reluctance by the mental health community to extend their methods into the political sphere, the project need not be a utopian one, and could begin to function as soon as a small number of people could be found to begin monitoring major nations. Unlike other proposals which have been made for joint "Crisis Control Centers" between nations—proposals which require the agreement of several governments to work—the Nuclear Tensions Monitoring Center will probably decide to avoid government sponsorship at the start, under the principle that people in government often act as delegates of war wishes rather than as representatives of the reality principle. In fact, government funding would likely be terminated even if initially obtained, as I personally discovered in a minor incident recently. One of President Reagan's speech writers had attended some workshops of the Washington, D.C. branch of our Institute and was impressed enough with the technique of fantasy analysis to have offered the use of the White House computer for analyzing presidential speeches over the past several decades. When, however, my book, *Reagan's America*—which uses fantasy analysis on Reagan's speeches—was sent to him at the White House, the offer was quickly withdrawn. As Bion once put it, "people do not generally appreciate the investigation of the deity whose cult is at the time flourishing."[8]

The establishment of a Nuclear Tensions Monitoring Center, I believe, need only depend upon the energy, courage and resources of those in the mental health profession and social sciences who are vitally concerned with the avoidance of nuclear war. Because the Monitoring Center would involve analyzing contemporary government and media publications and broadcasts from many countries, it would ideally need a branch in each of the nuclear nations to do its task fully. Yet it could begin to function with only one center, probably in America, where the mental health profession is most developed. In one sense, the Monitoring Center would have the same relationship to governments and nations that a "suicide hot line" at a mental health center has to its suicidal clients: that of interpreting and assisting those who are about to act out suicidal wishes. The Monitoring Center would concentrate on a continuous analysis of the rise and fall of violent and paranoid imagery in the speeches and media of the nuclear nations, with the hope that before long an actual index of national war tensions could be constructed which would be able to warn people when and why nations are escalating their violent group-fantasies.[9]

Needless to say, the realities as well as the fantasies of nuclear war could also be studied at the Monitoring Center, including developments in nuclear armaments and their means of delivery and deployment. It certainly is relevant to our study of nuclear dangers that massive first-strike weapons are currently in place, that first-strike scenarios are being officially considered, that the Soviet Union and the United States are deploying cruise missiles in great numbers which are so small that they are invulnerable to detection and thus make all treaty verification impossible, that six-minute delivery systems have transferred world-destruction decisions to computers, and that Star Wars deployments threaten to reduce the

hair-trigger time from six minutes to milliseconds.[10] Yet the present realities of our nuclear posture are now so horrendous that even Star Wars
deployments will not increase real dangers by much. We unfortunately
have already put the Doomsday Machine in place, and it is set to go off at
the slightest touch. The only questions which remain to be answered are
who will set it off and when. Thus questions of motivation, not mainly
those of reality, will ultimately be the focus for the Monitoring Center,
and people who are trained in psychology, not in the physical sciences, will
be the main researchers at the Center.

One of the first discoveries which is likely to be made by these researchers is how little writing has been published to date on motivations for war.
Nuclear war motivations in particular are virtually a taboo subject in the
psychological and social sciences. There are, of course, endless numbers of
books and articles discussing one nuclear posture as compared to another
or analyzing survivability under various scenarios or relating histories of
nuclear negotiations.[11] Yet none of them focuses on motivation, even
amongst the best of them. Furthermore, virtually every book on nuclear
war which had been written previously was rendered meaningless by the
findings of Carl Sagan, Paul Ehrlich and others demonstrating that the
setting off of as little as 100 megatons out of the 12,000 available of the
nuclear arsenal would produce so much smoke and debris that it would
reduce the sun's light to 17 percent of normal, possibly destroying the
earth's ecological system and thus all human life.[12] Once this has been
said, the conclusion follows that there is no rational use whatsoever for
nuclear weapons on either side. Every scenario which we continue to
seriously entertain, whether labeled "offensive" or "defensive," is a
scenario for world suicide. Our continued discussion of survival strategies
and possible "uses" of nuclear arms only contributes to delusional survival fantasies, in much the same manner as people who are about to com-
mit suicide often imagine themselves surviving their own death in order to
watch others mourning for them and loving them at last. Both nations and
individuals try suicide only when they feel very "bad," imagining they are
killing only a part of themselves, with the "good" part surviving to be
loved.

Fantasies of surviving nuclear war are extraordinarily widespread.
This is understandable, since they form the main condition for the
underlying fantasy of an earth cleansed of evil, i.e., cleansed of com-
munism or of capitalism, in the case of U.S. and Soviet fantasies. This
fantasy is identical with that held by those Germans who promised a happy post-war world once Europe was cleansed of Jews. Surviving after a
nuclear holocaust is an explicit doctrine of major powers today.[13] In
America, it is called the Single Integrated Operational Plan (SIOP),[14]
and it has been called "one of the nation's most carefully guarded
secrets."[15] The American President, Vice-President and many of the

cabinet members have publicly said in the past that a nuclear war is "survivable." Key officials regularly go through exercises in which they pretend they are flying over an incinerated America, in a plane appropriately given the narcissistic code name of "Looking Glass," while giving orders for nuclear retaliation, ignoring the fact that the plane would soon have to rejoin the rest of us in the lethal atmosphere below.[16] Survival after victory in a nuclear war is currently being argued with increasing frequency and seriousness in the literature of international relations,[17] despite occasional denials by national leaders of the possibility of nuclear victory. Embedded in the arguments for these survival scenarios are fantasies of the potency-restoring capacity of war. The notion of war as having a sexual component is not a new one. As a recent *Esquire* magazine cover proclaimed, war is "a sexual turn-on...the secret love of a man's life...the closest thing to what childbirth is for women."[18] Candid reports by veterans of recent wars are filled with admissions that "when you're in the airplane, and you fire a rocket, and you hear that shoosh leave your wing, then all of a sudden it hits. POW. It's like an orgasm," or "carrying a gun constantly was like having a permanent hard on."[19] Instances could be multiplied indefinitely.

Of course, the days are past when leaders could openly espouse the notion that war was, as one American official said during World War I, a "restoration of national virility.... There is not a weakness in American life that it would not strengthen."[20] Nevertheless, group-fantasies of the restoration of virility and fears of impotence still underlie much of international relations today. American policies are presently dominated by notions that proclaim that "soft" Europeans are about to push America into a castrating "Munich" humiliation—when the "effeminate" British capitulated to the "macho" Germans—and that America must instead "make the Commies blink" as they did in the Cuban Missile Crisis. Though not as explicitly stated as this, all these ideas are quite widespread today. It is the same group-fantasy as that expressed by the old Spanish proverb that "when a nation shows a civilized horror of war...God changes its sex, despoils it of its common mark of virility, changes it into a feminine nation, and sends conquerers to ravage it of its honor."[21] Rape or be raped (and it is often homosexual rape that is envisioned) is the operative fantasy behind much of what purports to be serious discussion of international affairs today.

Because this kind of symbolism is so explicit in world affairs, I have found little difficulty in training others in the techniques of fantasy analysis, once they are already familiar with unconscious symbolism in dreams and other sources of individual fantasy. Political symbolism is rarely subtle. When nuclear powers go to disarmament meetings, cartoons on both sides show them comparing gigantic phallic missiles, conspicuously erect between their legs. When Reaganomics proposes cuts in social services, cartoons show babies being thrown into the fires of a sacrificial pit. When war is being contemplated, as currently (early 1985) in Nicaragua, headlines scream about the "TRADE WARS," "TRAFFIC WARS," "PRICE WARS" and "WORD WARS" which come to dominate the media rhetoric, and the entire nation becomes fascinated with the actions of a vigilante subway murderer. The President, in turn, responds by adopting the words of a film vigilante ("Make my day") and then visits a cemetery with SS graves. The fantasies conveyed in such dream imagery usually do not need extensive interpretation; all they need is to be viewed as *wishes*. A dozen cartoons showing Reagan as a Nazi leader means we want him to be our Nazi leader and take us to war. When is he portrayed in hundreds of cartoons as a gun-carrying vigilante or as a gun-shooting cowboy, the analyst must suspect that wishes are being floated in our collective fantasy system, just as they were when, before Vietnam, hundreds of cartoons showed Barry Goldwater (the evil double of Johnson) as similarly trigger-happy.

The main problem I have found with fantasy analysis is that it takes an enormous amount of courage to persist in doing it. Most of the countertransference problems of the analyst revolve around fears of engulfment by the very powerful fantasies being investigated. Courage is additionally needed to withstand the inevitable attacks by people who with great conviction hold these group-fantasies and share in their defensive systems, and who imagine any analysis of them makes you dangerous to their well-being. This can be especially difficult for professionals whose colleagues disagree with their discoveries; those who join the Monitoring Center should be prepared for possible challenges by these colleagues about the legitimacy of their activities. This, of course, is hardly surprising, as some of our deepest fears and most infantile violent wishes lie behind our shared group-fantasies, and other people's transference feelings should be expected to be correspondingly hostile. Researchers whose own fantasies and fears have not been thoroughly analyzed or who need regular peer approval to function will find it hard to stay with such a Center for long.

Unfortunately, interpreting international fantasy systems will be a bit like trying to do therapy with a family who walks into a therapist's office fully armed with many kinds of weapons and who is prepared only to talk about which one has the largest guns. Interpretation in such an atmosphere must proceed cautiously and must begin with extensive analysis of defensive layers. Nations, like individual family members, assign each other roles in their family systems, designating which nation is to be the scapegoat, which is to be the violent one, which is to make decisions while denying responsibility, and so on. As psychohistorian David Beisel has shown,[22] this is how World War II was brought about by the European family of nations, with England playing "controlling mother," Germany playing "bad adolescent," France playing "rejected child," Czechoslovakia playing "the suicide," and so on. Beisel's analysis shows that the main challenge of the Allies in starting the war was how to disunite sufficiently enough to allow an initially weaker Germany to achieve some victories. Because the group processes in international relations resemble individual family dynamics so closely, researchers will have to be thoroughly familiar with family psychodynamics in order to be able to monitor the unconscious messages being circulated amongst the nuclear powers.

To refuse to apply to the subject of nuclear madness all the knowledge which we have accumulated on madness since Freud would be unforgivable. Happily, the mental health community has recently shown some interest in the nuclear threat after decades of staying mainly aloof from it. As one example, the latest American Orthopsychiatric Association's annual meeting recently featured seven papers on the subject. One, entitled "The Nuclear Threat: One Community's Approach," described a small group of mental health professionals who began by noting pervasive nuclear fears in their patients, then went on to organize discussion groups which explored common feelings, and then finally formed several quite effective anti-war centers.[23] Yet all of these activities involved mental health professionals in organization and protest movements in much the same ways as other professionals, such as the Physicians for Social Responsibility, were already doing. As necessary as this may be, it does not really use the specific training and expertise of the mental health professional. Perhaps the assumption has been that decoding the fantasies embedded in political dialogue was wholly different from interpreting the dreams or free associations of individuals. Yet one must wonder if, after a Monitoring Center were established and motivations for nuclear war were better understood, many of the present anti-war activities might seem ineffective, and others might be devised to replace or supplement them which have a better psychological basis.

Whatever the ultimate use which governments, groups and individuals around the world may eventually make of the Center, the initial task must be the organization of a group of mental health and social science professionals which will begin the difficult task of gathering, organizing and interpreting the mass of material needed to understand our present nuclear situation. Those who finally decide to join the Center will be motivated not by monetary or career goals, but ultimately only out of love...for our children, for our world and for ourselves.

FOOTNOTES

1. George F. Kennan, "The Nuclear Standoff," *Current,* September 1981, p. 3.
2. These analyses can be found in Lloyd deMause, *Foundations of Psychohistory.* N.Y.: Creative Roots, 1982; David Beisel, *The Dance of Death: An Inquiry Into the Origins*

58 LLOYD DEMAUSE

of the Second World War, forthcoming; Lloyd deMause, *Reagan's America.* N.Y.: Creative Roots, 1984; and articles in *The Journal of Psychohistory.*

3. This literature appears in the *Journal of Psychohistory,* the *Journal of Psychoanalytic Anthropology,* and other publications of the Psychohistory Press and the International Psychohistorical Association. For information on The Institute for Psychohistory and its publications, write the Institute for Psychohistory, 2315 Broadway, New York, New York 10024.

4. A more detailed statement of the psychogenic theory can be found in deMause, *Foundations* and *Reagan's America,* and in the forthcoming book by deMause, *The War Trance.*

5. For the regression of the psychotic process, see John Frosch, *The Psychotic Process.* N.Y.: International Universities Press, 1983, pp. 63ff.

6. Those who wish to inquire about joining this project may request information by writing The Nuclear Tensions Monitoring Center, Room 300, 2315 Broadway, New York, New York 10024, or by calling (212) 873-5900.

7. William Lury, *Beyond the Hotline: How Crisis Control Can Prevent Nuclear War.* Boston: Houghton Mifflin, 1985.

8. W.R. Bion, *Experience in Groups, and Other Papers.* N.Y.; Ballantine Books, 1974, p. 87.

9. The first index of national war tensions was in Ole R. Holsti and Robert C. North, "The history of human conflict." In Elton B. McNeil, ed., *The Nature of Human Conflict.* Englewood Cliffs, N.J.: Prentice-Hall, 1965, pp. 166ff.

10. See such analyses as Helen Caldicott, *Missile Envy: The Arms Race & Nuclear War.* N.Y.: William Morrow & Co., 1984 and Daniel Ford, "A Reporter at Large (U.S. Command and Control, Part II—The Button," *The New Yorker,* April 8, 1985, pp. 49-91.

11. See for example Robert Scheer, *With Enough Shovels: Reagan, Bush and Nuclear War.* Updated Edition. N.Y.: Vintage Books, 1983; Louis Rene Beres, *Apocalypse: Nuclear Catastrophe in World Politics.* Chicago: University of Chicago Press, 1980; Emma Rothschild, "The Delusions of Deterrence," *The New York Review of Books,* April 15, 1983, pp. 40ff; and Joel Kovel, *Against the State of Nuclear Terror.* Boston: South End Press, 1983.

12. Paul R. Erlich and others, "Long-term Biological Consequences of Nuclear War." *Science* 22 (1983), 1293-1300. For a bibliograpchy of works disputing this conclusion, see Richard Routley, "Metaphysical Fallout From the Nuclear Predicament." *Philosophy & Social Criticism* 3(1984):19-34.

13. Scheer, *With Enough Shovels,* cites dozens of examples of these survivability beliefs, as does Strobe Talbott, *Deadly Gambits: The Reagan Administration and the Stalemate in Nuclear Arms Control.* N.Y.: Knopf, 1984 and Edward Zuckerman, *The Day After World War III: The U.S. Government's Plans for Surviving a Nuclear War.* N.Y.: Viking, 1984.

14. See Peter Pringle and William Arkin, *SIOP: The Secret U.S. Plan for Nuclear War.* N.Y.: Norton, 1983.

15. Talbott, *Deadly Gambits,* p. 255.

16. The fantasy nature of the "Looking Glass" plans is explained in Ford, "A Reporter at Large," pp. 80-83.

17. As an example, see Colin S. Gray and Keith Payne, "Victory is Possible." *Foreign Policy,* Summer 1980, pp. 14-27. The subject is fully discussed in Spurgeon M. Keeny, Jr. and Wolfgang K.H. Panofsky, "MAD versus NUTS," in William P. Bundy, editor, *The Nuclear Controversy: A Foreign Affairs Reader.* N.Y.: New American Library, 1985, pp. 3-20.

18. *Esquire,* November 1984.

19. Loren Baritz, *Backfire: A History of How American Culture Led Us Into Vietnam and Made Us Fight The Way We Did*. N.Y.: William Morrow, 1984, p. 53.
20. Cited in Caldicott, *Missile Envy,* p. 299.
21. Ibid.
22. Beisel, *Dance of Death.*
23. Judith Ashway, Arnold Kerzner and Martin Norman, "The Nuclear Threat: One Community's Approach." 62nd Annual Meeting, American Orthopsychiatric Association, New York City, April 21, 1985.

5

Psychotherapy, Countertransference and the Nuclear Arms Race

Adela Wilkeson, M.D.

It is a heart,
This holocaust I walk in,
O golden child the world will kill and eat.

"Mary's Song," Sylvia Plath[1]

Introduction

Though generally concerned about the nuclear arms race, most psychotherapists rarely discuss this subject with their patients. The main goal of this chapter is to alert mental health professionals to the likelihood that countertransference resistances impede clinically needed responsivity to nuclear themes. This hypothesis is based on three observations: first, the distinctive difference in my clinical experiences with this issue since I became fully aware of the nature of the nuclear threat three-and-a-half years ago; second, the escalating threat of nuclear annihilation evokes intense emotions which most people defend against through unconscious defense mechanisms commonly referred to as nuclear numbing—psychotherapists have no immunity to the power of these individual and collective efforts to avoid emotional openness to the possibility of nuclear holocaust; and third, when given the opportunity, patients do readily discuss many concerns and feelings about this issue.

Among the first of my patients to raise the theme of nuclear war was a teenager hospitalized for treatment of a psychotic illness. During the second year of our work she introduced me to the following lines of a song from the album and movie, *Pink Floyd The Wall:*[2]

> Mother do you think they'll drop the bomb
> Mother should I build a wall...
> Mother should I trust the government...
> Mother am I really dying
>
> Hush now baby don't you cry
> Mama's gonna make all of your
> Nightmares come true
> Mama's gonna put all her fears into you...
> Of course mam'll help build the wall...

She told me the album was her favorite. She listened to it often because it helped her feel sad. The reason for her attraction to this rock production seemed readily identifiable as I listened to the lyrics and later viewed the film. The work portrays the psychotic decompensation of its rock-star protagonist. Discussing the patient's identification with Pink Floyd deepened my alliance with this disturbed adolescent.

The year this work took place was 1982. Early in 1982 I joined Physicians for Social Responsibility and began the process of breaking through my hitherto intact nuclear numbing. Learning about the actual nature of current nuclear arsenals[3], [4], [5] the unprecedented medical and ecologic consequences that would result from their utilization[6], [7], [8] and the history behind treatment negotiation failures [9], [10], [11] has deeply affected my life. I experienced the crisis of awareness and compelling feelings described later in this chapter. Prior to this time I would not have recognized that the central theme of *Pink Floyd the Wall* is the madness of the threat of nuclear holocaust: "Mother do you think they'll drop the bomb." My noting this theme became the first of many discussions of the realities of the arms race and reasons why nuclear fears would become particularly intense at different times in this patient's life.

Before breaking through my nuclear numbing, I had not heard a single reference to the nuclear issue by my patients. Since the change in my awareness, I have heard references to it from the majority. In informal conversations with colleagues I find that my experience is not the norm. A brief questionnaire survey of 39 psychotherapists inquiring about clinical experience with this subject confirmed this impression. The majority report concern regarding the arms race but little to no experience with patients referring to it. One colleague, Stephen Armstrong, Ph.D. (who has graciously provided clinical material from his separate psychotherapy practice and has been fully aware of the nuclear threat for many years), also frequently hears references to the subject. Twenty-six of our 37 patients (70%) have raised the subject in some manner.

The most compelling evidence supporting the hypothesis that therapists are not responding to deeply felt patient needs to talk about the arms race (the intense emotions it evokes and its associated intrapsychic meanings) is what patients actually say. Thus detailed case reports will be presented both in the text and Appendix in order to provide the reader with examples of the many ways in which patients deal with the subject.

The definition of countertransference being used in this discussion is the broader sense of any emotions evoked by dealing with a particular subject.[12] It is important for therapists to appreciate the difficulty of openly contemplating the possibility of nuclear holocaust. Struggling with these feelings is not the result of unresolved early childhood conflicts. It is an unavoidable part of living with the most overwhelming reality mankind has ever faced. The emotional impact of living with the nuclear threat must not be underestimated. Before presenting case material and the therapists' survey findings, literature on psychological consequences of living with the constant threat of annihilation will be reviewed.

Living with Nuclear Terror

The phenomenon of nuclear numbing has been well described.[13], [14], [15], [16], [17], [18], [19] Clinicians are familiar with the psychological defense mechanisms involved: denial, rationalization, intellectualization, isolation of affect, displacement, dehumanization, etc. These mechanisms block conscious awareness of the nuclear threat to prevent experiencing the seemingly unbearable emotions evoked by consideration of the possibility of annihilation.

The arms race has a profound impact on our lives. The 1964 G.A.P.[20] report summarizes a number of psychological effects. For example, self-directed dehumanization involves the closing off of whole clusters of human affects and states of mind: fear, compassion, guilt, shame, indignation, rage. Conscious experience becomes compartmentalized, considerations of job efficiency become primary and erode compassion for human suffering. The capacity to feel and act like a human being diminishes. Healthy aspects of an individual's self-image such as courage, autonomy, power, responsibility, and sacrifice are lost. The passive group-based paranoid projection of responsibility for existing dangers and malice onto the enemy is a related process. Another numbing reaction is depression. Sixty percent of those polled in a 1982 media survey indicated that the arms race is too depressing to think about.

The existence of psychological defense mechanisms does not fully explain the process of nuclear numbing. On an individual basis, when serious life-threatening events occur, most people are able to overcome such defenses and respond adaptively: for example, undergoing extensive medical treatment for a malignant illness.

Some have suggested that the threat of annihilation is "unthinkable" or "unimaginable." The problem is the opposite. Doctors, scientists, military and governmental strategic planners have imagined and described in great detail the likely aftermath of a nuclear war. Fantasies of annihilation characterize emotional conflicts of the earliest stages of psychological life. These conflicts are resolved by the development of stable object ties.[21], [22] The fact that nuclear weapons threaten to destroy all bonds, past, present, and future, may be the most significant determinant of nuclear numbing. A collusive conspiracy of silence and sanctioning of unfounded omnipotent beliefs block recognition of our absolute vulnerability to these weapons.[23] Such false beliefs include survivability of a nuclear exchange and the illusion that national security can be enhanced by pursuing unattainable "superiority" in nuclear weaponry. The emotions numbed by these defenses resonate with early life fears of similar vulnerability now an external reality rather than solely a childhood nightmare.

Extinction would bring about what Jonathan Schell terms the "second death": the death of all future generations.[24] Our connectedness with the past and all present ties would also end. As Robert Lifton notes, until present times, death has always occurred in the context of continuity.[25] Aspirations and interest in contributing to the greater well-being of mankind, labeled by Erik Erikson[26] as generativity, are important elements of adult life. The threat of nuclear holocaust deeply disrupts these essential bonds to past, present, and future humanity.

When past and future are jeopardized, more is sought from present experience than can be realized. The hedonistic tendencies of the 1960s and the rapid shift to frenetic investment in hard work and the highly competitive attitudes of the 1970s belie the underlying meaninglessness of our activity. The increasingly narcissistic orientation of our society; lack of trust in and commitment to enduring relationships; seeking immediate pleasures through drugs, more expressive forms of dance and music, and the sexual revolution; the re-emergence of apocalyptic religious cults and interests in mysticism, all become more understandable in the light of the ever-present threat that holds our world in terror.[27] In Jonathan Schell's words:

> The approach of extinction drives love back into its perishable moment and in so doing tends to break up love's longer attachment...love...has tended to withdraw to a

mental plane peculiarly its own, where it becomes an ever
more solitary affair: impersonal, detached, pornographic.[28]

Nuclear numbing is not impregnable. Due to the gravity of the nuclear
threat and the intense emotions evoked in facing this reality, the
breakdown of nuclear numbing can precipitate a major life crisis. This
crisis of awareness is similar to reactions to a catastrophic event. Initially
people feel shocked or stunned.[29] This gives way to intense feelings of
terror. Despair, grief, and depression follow. Over a period that generally lasts several months, episodes of anxiety characterized by intrusive
thoughts recur. A subjective sense of incapacity to bear the feelings and
the belief that this is a result of some personal psychological weakness
are typical during these months. Close relationships with family
members and friends who individuals ordinarily turn to for support can
be strained if the concerns and feelings are not appreciated.

Eventually these feelings can be worked through, facilitating the
mobilization of hope, anger, and creative energy. Some people will feel a
tremendous compulsion to work on the issue. Though the all-
encompassing intensity of the breakdown of nuclear numbing can be
resolved, it is not possible to again establish a sense of equilibrium vis-a-
vis this issue. Compulsions to do more, frustrations and guilt about personal limits continue to affect persons who have the courage to remain
open.

Basic principles of crisis intervention can help attenuate the severity of
the crisis of awareness. Most people feel a pressing need to talk about the
issue and will do so readily with others who understand that group involvement provides support.[30, 31] Learning the facts and contributing to
the disarmament effort enhance feelings of mastery. Such activities also
help prevent reversion to earlier avoidance or entrenchment in hopeless
despondency.

Descriptive reports thus note adverse emotional reactions associated
with living under the shadow of an ever-expanding doomsday machine.
Unfortunately, these discussions have not been followed by systematic
epidemiologic and/or clinical studies. What is the degree of subjective
distress associated with increasing awareness? What is the prevalence of
adult life crises of awareness associated with the breakdown of nuclear
numbing? What has helped people deal with these troublesome emotions? Are there identifiable constellations of attitudes that contribute to
the problem of passivity? Does the nuclear threat exacerbate other
clinical systems? A data base is urgently needed to discuss the best
clinical responses to these issues and to develop public educational services that will meet existing needs.

The few reported studies of children have value in this regard. They
reveal that early latency-age children are aware of nuclear weapons.

Videotaped interviews of normal U.S. and Soviet children and adolescents have captured the loneliness, isolation, and personal insignificance that are part of our nuclear era.[32], [22] Mack and Beardslee surveyed 1,151 children (mainly adolescents) between 1978 and 1980. Their results demonstrate the existence of considerable awareness and concern: "Our strongest finding, we feel, is a general unquiet or uneasiness about the future and about the present nature of nuclear weapons and nuclear power."[34]

These results parallel Escalona's 1960 findings where 70 percent of the children who were asked about their thoughts about the future, without any specific references made by the inquirer to nuclear weapons, spontaneously raised concerns about the subject.[35] How subjectively disturbing these concerns are for children, as well as their impact on personality development, warrants further attention. Children lack adult psychological mechanisms that help block open experiencing of nuclear terror. They need responsive parents who can acknowledge the realities of the arms race and genuinely assure them that everything possible is being done to change the situation. It is particularly true for children in this regard that actions speak louder than words.

Research Findings

I distributed a voluntary questionnaire at the 1984 meeting of the American Academy of Psychotherapists. Thirty-nine of the 134 registrants (29%) returned completed questionnaires, which is an acceptable return rate for this method.[36] The returned questionnaires are from an experienced group of psychotherapists (average in practice, 15 years) who are engaged primarily in private practice from half- to full-time as psychiatrists (N = 8), clinical psychologists (N = 20), or psychiatric social workers (N = 11). These psychotherapists describe themselves as "concerned about the nuclear arms race" and see it as a "very serious issue" (N = 13). Another one-third have attended conferences or seminars about nuclear weapons or arms control (N = 15). Only four psychotherapists (10%) say that they have made "no particular effort" to inform themselves about nuclear weapons control. Six describe themselves as "deeply concerned," having gone through a period of emotional upheaval and/or having made a commitment to work on the issue actively.

Results

These experienced and concerned psychotherapists report that patients rarely if ever broach the problems of nuclear weapons in psychotherapy either directly (for instance, by asking a question or initiating a discussion) or indirectly (for instance, by talking about television news, current events, or a "passing thought"). Ten therapists say that patients have "never" mentioned the problem of nuclear weapons; another 21 say that fewer than "one in five patients" ever have made a direct reference to nuclear weapons or arms control. Only four hear direct references by 60 percent of their patients and five hear indirect references from 60 to 80 percent of their patients. If a patient does mention nuclear weapons, nearly half (17/39) of the psychotherapists report that they ask for further information or thoughts from patients, but a significant number of psychotherapists (8/39) say that nuclear weapons are a "political subject" and should not be discussed at any length.

Case Material

Over the past three years I have seen 19 long-term patients. The duration of therapy ranges from 10 years to one year. The average number of weekly appointments is between two to three. Thirteen of these 19 patients have dealt with the subject. These include two borderline and one psychotic adolescents and two psychotic, four borderline, and four neurotic adults. Three psychotic, one severely disturbed borderline, and two neurotic adults have not referred to the issue.

Clinically, during most of the hours when I first heard reference to the arms race, I noted the comment and asked if the patient had further thoughts about the subject. Generally patients spoke without hesitation and at some length of the range of feelings described above. Patients whose references were indirect were less expressive initially, although months later, they explicitly raised the subject. My responses have involved confirming the realistic nature of their concerns, describing the course of feelings generally experienced by those who begin to think about the danger, and how these feelings can be handled. I also mentioned my disarmament work. I explained my reason for doing so was to underscore the seriousness of the issue to reinforce my availability to discuss associated thoughts and/or feelings.[a]

Two case reports follow. Additional clinical vignettes appear in the Appendix.

Case 1 (A.B.)

I began seeing this married borderline woman in her thirties once a week in the spring of 1980. Severe borderline pathology had presented incapacitating symptoms for 10 years. Work with several therapists and brief hospitalizations did not change the course of her illness and thus necessitated referral for long-term hospitalization. Two years of inpatient treatment helped A.B. engage in therapy and begin to alter her life course. She was referred to me because the therapist she began seeing during that hospitalization was moving out of town.

Approximately two months prior to terminating with the previous therapist, A.B. made a suicide gesture. We reviewed this incident in the initial weeks of therapy, but I heard no reference to nuclear-related concerns at that time. A.B. suggested that the precipitant involved an embarrassing incident that had occurred between herself and her father for whom she was working in a family business. My noting the connection between the gesture and the anticipated loss of the therapist helped her work through this significant loss.

The first reference I heard to the nuclear issue occurred in June 1982. When I noted a passing comment and asked if she had further thoughts about the subject, she readily revealed many intense feelings which had troubled her intermittently for some time. As she continued, I learned for the first time that she had been involved in disarmament work over the past two years. Her family's business, which involves an aspect of public relations work, had in fact contributed to the development of one of the national symposia held early in 1980 by Physicians for Social Responsibility. A.B. had attended this conference and vividly recalled waves of terror, nightmares and feelings of despair overwhelming her for several weeks afterward. She did not recall discussing these feelings with her former therapists. Significantly, the suicide gesture noted above occurred six weeks after the symposium.

The following week she continued to discuss feelings about the arms race that had been rekindled by her attendance at a disarmament conference over the weekend. This was followed by new history about her family's long-standing involvement in liberal politics including latency-years memories of a paranoid atmosphere regarding any discussion of such interests outside the home during the McCarthy era. These memories shed light upon the intermeshed nature of A.B.'s family.

The next reference occurred 14 months later (August 1983). In the interim she increased therapy to twice a week to work further on separating from her family. Unlike the June 1982 discussion, which seemed prompted by public attention to the arms race, the August reference occurred in the context of A.B. making meaningful steps toward establishing greater authority for herself within the family business. The external context for the reference involved the patient's interest in increasing the priority of disarmament-related work within the business. Her heightened anxieties were also related to the changes she was making regarding her role in relation to her father. Shortly thereafter the patient reported two frightening dreams that confirmed this association. The first involved her taking over her father's position as head of their business. In the other she was wandering aimlessly in the aftermath of a nuclear war.

Over the next several weeks we reviewed increased feelings of compulsion to devote more time to the arms race. It was possible to distinguish the genuinely compelling nature of living with the threat of nuclear war from her characterologic tendency to overwork. This separation of internal and external motivations helped her set realistic limits on her work and begin to give more attention to meeting her needs through involvement with people and activities that gave her pleasure.

Attendance at a disarmament conference in early October 1983, the death of Marines in Beirut, and the invasion of Grenada prompted further waves of intrusive thoughts involving nuclear holocaust. A.B. benefitted from each discussion of these feelings and learned to accept that such intermittent heightened fears are normal.

Among the troublesome feelings she reported during this time was the difficulty of not being able to feel understood by her husband because of his general denial of existing dangers. She valued hearing that many people who are open to the subject are similarly disturbed by the ubiquity of denial and despondence. I noted that feelings of isolation are heightened by such contrasting attitudes and that differences in openness to the issue between those we are closest to, can be particularly stressful. She recognized an ongoing need to be close to others who share her concerns and made plans to have lunch with friends involved in disarmament work. She subsequently sought a support group to be with during the movie *The Day After,* shown nationally on American Broadcasting Company television, November 20, 1983. Though she feared the film would again be disruptive, she reported little difficulty afterward. She noted instead that she had become more able to confront the issue without being overwhelmed and said that the film had had a positive impact in that it helped decrease her husband's level of denial.

Case 2 (C.D.)

I began seeing this single woman seven years ago at age 19 when she dropped out of college due to incapacitating depression with suicidal ideation. She has a borderline personality disorder with depressive features. Seven months of hospitalization were followed by one-and-a-half years of day hospital care along with two years residence in a halfway house. Despite severe pathology, she has made steady progress in three-times-per-week psychotherapy. This case summary is rather lengthy, in part because of C.D.'s remarkable capacity to be introspective and to articulate aspects of her internal emotional life.

Unlike my work with other patients, I first mentioned the subject of nuclear weapons with C.D. During the early years of our work she found it easier to endure times I was away if I told her briefly where I was going and what I would be doing. In June 1982 it was necessary to reschedule

three Saturday appointments because of my involvement in weekend disarmament programs. She expressed fears that I was taking time off
casually and did not appreciate her need for constancy in our relationship. After exploring these fears and associated feelings, I told her the
reason I needed to reschedule. I explained that it was not an easy decision
and said it was only because of the significance of the nuclear issue that I
had decided to disrupt my clinical hours. She accepted this without apparent difficulty and continued to discuss her current life issues.

Seven months later, in January 1983, C.D. spontaneously raised concerns about my disarmament work. Prior to a rescheduled Saturday appointment she said she feared that I would give up my practice to work
full time on the nuclear issue. (I did not share with her this time the fact
that it was a disarmament commitment that necessitated the change. I
did shortly thereafter discontinue Saturday hours to avoid this complica-
tion.) The next hour she angrily voiced objections to my having
introduced the subject of nuclear weapons into our work and insisted
that it was only because she knew of my disarmament commitment that
she was having fears of abandonment. She resisted acknowledging the
fact that such fears were typical responses to changes in our schedule as
well as to periods of growth. This in fact was a time when she was making substantial gains vis-à-vis aspects of her femininity and relationships
with men. During the next hour she focused on fears of losing her
boyfriend without again mentioning the nuclear theme.

Four months later, during another period of progress, the subject
came up again. Shortly after an interruption, she had new insights into
her relationship with her sister. These were followed by childhood
memories of times she was petrified with the fear that her father was going to kill her during one of his episodic outbursts of primitive rage. Two
interviews later she raised fears of losing me. Toward the end of that interview she angrily insisted that these feelings had been prompted by the
fact that I was wearing a PSR pin. She felt this was insensitive to her expressed desire for me not to make any further reference to the arms race.
Though I noted that the reasons for her anger were multidetermined, I
did acknowledge the validity of her complaint about the pin. (I had worn
it for a speaking engagement earlier in the day and had not thought to
take it off. I have not worn it during clinical hours again.)

Progress was again occurring when the arms race was next mentioned
six months later. The change in the nature of this and subsequent discussions of the arms race seemed related to the fact that C.D. had developed
the capacity to identify that she constantly lived with intense anxiety
and/or terror. Immediately after she read about the death of Marines in
Beirut, she became overwhelmed with fears that the world might im-
minently be destroyed by nuclear war. She spoke of these feelings spontaneously at the beginning of our next appointment. She shared for the

first time that similar waves of terror had occurred many times in the past. She also observed that she was particularly vulnerable to such reactions because they mirrored her internal view of the world as being a very depressing and dangerous place.

During our next appointment she described experiencing the most overwhelming two days she had been through in several years. She had overeaten to the point of severe pain and had thoughts of suicide for the first time in over two years. She indicated that these feelings were a continuation of her reaction to the nuclear threat. She briefly again projected responsibility for the subject onto me but was able to go on with her own thoughts and feelings. She distinguished the ominous external threat of annihilation from internal fears of similar form and magnitude. She said the arms race made it extremely hard for her to feel hopeful as it reinforced a belief that nothing good could happen in her life and undermined her determination to sustain the work of therapy. Feelings of despair brought her to tears briefly during this and the next hour.

Her mood vacillated over the weekend. She was unable to sustain efforts to use newer ways to spend her time that helped her not "wallow in her misery." Sunday night she dreamt that I had left her with a muddled list of potential therapists. Review of the dream made it clear that her recent struggle with fears about nuclear war had also affected her sense of trust and constancy in our relationship. Going beyond renewed projections, she spoke of the destructiveness of nuclear weapons symbolically representing the rageful side of her ambivalent feelings being stirred up by therapy helping her to separate from her family.

Prior to the Beirut incident, C.D. had been in relatively good spirits. Though she attempted to push away her terror and tried to avoid any exposure to news media, she was unable to prevent a period of depression, withdrawal, and isolation. She felt that talking about the issue further with me would not help, but did respond favorably to my indicating that the feelings she was experiencing were normal responses to the arms race and could be worked through. This also helped her recognize that part of her regression had been prompted by the amount of progress she had been making for several months.

Several days before the showing of *The Day After,* still depressed, she dreamt that I was late to our appointment and that she overheard me talking to someone about the film. We had not discussed the film prior to this dream. I confronted her defensive suggestion that if I had not spoken of nuclear arms there would be nothing to be concerned about. We discussed briefly her viewing the film. She valued my encouraging her not to because it was not something she felt emotionally prepared to handle. The next week she described how difficult it was to avoid the movie. Awareness that it was going to be shown continued for her all day. In the evening she could hear muffled sounds from her landlords viewing it one floor below. She even received a rare phone call from her mother who asked, "Are you watching that horrible movie?" Her mother's devaluation, interestingly, prompted angry feelings regarding her mother's general inability to recognize things that were important in the world and that the patient cared about.

Despondency continued over the next few weeks. Toward the end of an hour (December 1983), after asking me not to comment further, she told me that the nuclear threat was continuing to preoccupy her and that it particularly came to mind when she tried to think about me. She accepted my initial comment that this in some way indicated her being out of touch with me as a supportive figure. I spoke of appreciating how difficult it was for her to discuss the nuclear issue and noted that I was making every effort to be conservative in my responses. She nodded recognition of this. I added that it was also difficult for her not to continue to think about the subject because the movie had prompted considerable public discussion of the arms race. She agreed that she had overheard several conversations about it.

In the following appointment her spirits were much better. She said this was because she had somehow been able to free herself from her preoccupations about the arms race. During the next hour, she said our discussing the fact that her fears of annihilation were so disturbing because they mirrored feelings from early childhood had made her feel hopeful, since she felt these were feelings she could eventually change. She also said hearing that everyone has to defend against directly feeling the emotions evoked by the nuclear reality had been helpful.

A level II pap smear and an impending rare family reunion prompted the next references to nuclear arms four months later. The medical news was overwhelming and regressive. Yearning for her mother became intense. Fears that something terrible was going to happen to her family merged with fears of environmental pollutants and with the threat of nuclear war. With help she was again able to appreciate how external threats parallel childhood fears about her family.

Over the next three months there were a few passing references to "the fears" still being present to some degree. On a less frequent basis such comments continue to occur. The understading between us now is that we will only discuss these thoughts vis-à-vis their symbolic internal meaning unless something occurs that prompts a desire to discuss aspects of the arms race directly.

The subject came up more explicitly again in June 1984. C.D. had decided to look for a more demanding job involving career aspirations that she had not felt prepared to handle earlier. An interview with a potential employer went very well. This initially excited her and reinforced her sense of interest in this career. However, the next day she was overcome with fear. The threat of nuclear holocaust became terrifyingly real. Though describing her feelings without hesitation, she initially again said that she did not want to talk about it. I asked why. She responded, "You always reinforce the reality of my fears." I noted that this was not true, adding that this is but one of many ideas of death and destruction that constantly plague her. She said, "I know but it gives me something real to attach them to." I then noted that these feelings were coming up at a time of significant change, which she readily acknowledged as a repetitive pattern. She then spoke for the first time of some ethical concerns about staying in her current job because her employers dealt with many aspects of the military and arms industry. I asked about this concern, wondering out loud with her if it might be related to the fact that her father's work as an engineer involved nuclear technology. She said she did not know, "but I don't want to feel guilty that the money paying for my therapy is coming from the military; I didn't have a choice."

We continued to talk more about her parents and her job search. She felt very good that evening with thoughts about how far she had come and how much she had changed and was not like her parents. She missed the next appointment because of an opportunity to visit with a friend who was in town unexpectedly. During the next hour she first told me of her positive feelings. She then revealed that over the past week her fears of nuclear annihilation had persisted "like never before." She said that talking about it on Monday had not been problematic for her and spontaneously commented that the missed session did not involve a conscious desire to avoid these feelings. We again discussed both the need to separate the external reality from its internal symbolic meaning and the connection for her with fears of abandonment stirred up by change. She went on to say that what she had been feeling totally paralleled her early childhood experiences; i.e., how she felt she had to constantly worry about her parents to prevent something ominous from happening.

She had a good weekend. On Monday she spoke of recognizing how she could be a separate person and make life meaningful for herself. The intensity of her panicky feelings had subsided. With a genuinely new and deeper positive feeling about life, she said that there were many "bad things" in the world including nuclear arms, but the way people can live with such realities was to have "things" that were meaningful to them.

There were two subsequent references to the nuclear issue. One occurred during a period of significant change (March 1985). Her specific words involved reading about many threatening events in the newspaper. She did not identify the fact that Congress had that day passed legislation to fund more MX missiles. I suspected she knew this but was afraid of directly dealing with increased fears about the progression of the arms race.

Several weeks later, after she had learned that her sister, with whom she had been out of touch for years, had developed anorexia and required hospitalization, she experienced another wave of nuclear-related anxiety. On both of these occasions she identified without my assistance the connection between the resurfacing of fears of nuclear holocaust and her ongoing struggle with feelings of separation and abandonment. In June 1985, while experiencing a regressive period, she also mentioned an intensification of nuclear fears among many other symptoms.

Discussion

These patients' emotional responses to to the nuclear arms race are not unlike those of the general public. Most people have readily accessible feelings and will talk openly about them with others who can understand. The capacity of patients clearly to describe their feelings vis-à-vis the arms race has been striking in comparison to the emotional limitations they experience in other areas of their lives. This has been particularly true of adolescents who have also asked more questions. They openly seek to know if the nuclear situation really is as bad as they have feared and to confirm that their "nightmares" are not just another manifestation of their emotional problems. Drawing attention to the subject has not impeded or interfered with the therapeutic process.

Many of the initial references were explicit and spontaneous though made in passing rather than something being raised for discussion. Other initial comments were indirect. For the long-term patient whose initial comments were noted, subsequent discussion, occurring at times many months later, was more spontaneous. Increased public awareness of the arms race such as that generated by the Freeze Movement in the spring of 1982 and by the film *The Day After* prompted discussion of the issue. This has also been true of times of increased international tension such as the death of the Marines in Beirut and the invasion of Grenada. Comments on the subject occurred at other times as well. These references seemed more connected to events in the patients' personal lives.

It seems from this small sample (see also Appendix) that individuals experiencing life crises either due to external events or severely incapacitating psychopathology are unlikely to mention the threat of nuclear war. On the other hand, patients who have established a therapeutic alliance and achieved some degree of stability in their lives will convey a desire to address the subject.

Without additional clinical material, generalizations about the realms of intrapsychic symbolic meaning which the arms race might represent can only be speculative. The subject was often associated with times at which patients were struggling with separation and individuation, and who were making progress and thus experiencing feelings of abandonment. The threat to all object ties posed by nuclear weapons makes this understandable. These patients and others also raised the issue of personal crises or regression, either precipitated by external events or by the progression of their work in therapy.

A.B. and C.D. both experienced crises of awareness as a result of opening themselves to the realities of the arms race. The suicide attempt made by A.B. was undoubtedly related to her reaction to the symposium held by Physicians for Social Responsibility. Since this occurred prior to my own opening to the subject, this case most dramatically suggests that I did not hear references made by A.B. or other patients until I had worked through my own numbing defenses. A.B. and C.D. further demonstrate how the feelings associated with nuclear weapons can be worked through. In fact, for these two women (as can occur at times of crises), dealing with these feeling in therapy facilitated personal growth.

In describing her increased isolation and anguish secondary to the marked differences of her husband's openness to this issue, A.B. also highlights the importance of the support of significant others during times of emotional responsivity. A parallel exists between patient and therapist. The clinical material presented in this chapter suggests that patients will test the therapist's openness to this terrifying reality. The therapeutic alliance involves open acceptance and encouragement to verbalize feelings that elsewhere seem taboo. For most patients this testing will not be fully conscious. It occurs on the level of projective and introjective identification. Attentiveness and sanctioning must come from the therapist to provide patients with an opportunity to explore their thoughts and feelings openly.

Psychotherapists are not immune to nuclear numbing. An intellectual "awareness" of the threat of extinction does not constitute working through the profound emotions associated with this most central reality of our time. Therapists' avoidance of the subject parallels societal avoidance. We, however, have a unique responsibility vis-à-vis our patients (which exists independent of the "political" aspects of this problem and societal efforts to alter the course of the arms race). Working through one's own numbing defenses is the critical step therapists must take to help patients deal with this terrifying reality. We must take the responsibility of not unconsciously jeopardizing our patient's emotional well-being as the lines from Pink Floyd convey:

> Hush now baby don't you cry
> Mama's gonna make all of your
> Nightmares come true
> Mama's gonna put all her fears into you...
> Of course mam'll help build the wall...[37]

Once this step is taken, responding to patients' attempts to cope with the peril of the escalating arms race requires only the same basic skills as we utilize daily in helping patients with any emotionally troublesome issue.

In public presentations of some of the material in this chapter, the question has been asked as to whether my experiences may not be the result of countertransference difficulties that I am having with this subject. Self-analysis is a basic skill we must all develop and exercise continuously. I have not attempted to induce nor ignore patient concerns regarding the nuclear threat. I have most often been surprised when the references have occurred. The intensity of the emotions evoked by the nuclear reality may make it easier to say that the bearer of bad news is the source of the problem. Of course, further reflection on the particular countertransference pitfalls therapists face would indeed be of value. In her first psychiatric interview, Celia of T.S. Eliot's *The Cocktail Party* expresses sentiments that seem most apt in response to those who raise such questions regarding countertransference in its more narrow definition of problems particular to an individual therapist's unresolved intrapsychic conflict:

> ...first I must tell you
> That I should really *like* to think there's something
> wrong with me—
> Because, if there isn't, then there's something wrong,
> Or at least, very different from what it seemed to be,
> With the world itself—and that's much more frightening![38]

APPENDIX

CASE 3 (E.F.)

A married borderline woman with narcissistic features in her early thirties who has been in therapy for ten years made a spontaneous reference to the arms race in June of 1982. At that time she was recovering from eye surgery. This was a significant event in that she had focused for many months on her eye problems as being the principal obstacle preventing her from going ahead with her life. She began the hour expressing renewed resolve to work in therapy and overcome her borderline emotional difficulties. For no explicit reason she mentioned having heard Dr. Helen Caldicott speak, noting in particular Dr. Caldicott's statement that government officials should be examined by psychiatrists. I asked if she had further thoughts about the subject of nuclear weapons. She said that she did think about it and at times considered not having children because of the threat of nuclear holocaust.

I mentioned my involvement with the issue and indicated that it was certainly a subject we could discuss at any time. She asked if I knew Dr.

Caldicott. I noted her curiosity and told her ordinarily, as she knew, I did not speak of aspects of my personal life, but had made an exception in this case because I felt the seriousness of the nuclear threat warranted explicit acknowledgement.

E.F. tenaciously persists in spending a great deal of time elaborating fantasies about me. It is quite uncharacteristic and interesting that she has not done this with regard to my nuclear work. She did ask in a relatively appropriate manner if I was going to a conference sponsored by International Physicians for the Prevention of Nuclear War (IPPNW), in June 1983. This inquiry was made at a time of some progress, which continued to be the focus of our hour. The only other reference involved several nightmares she had had at another period of progress. The dreams and other content of the hour seemed to involve intense separation anxiety.

CASE 4 (G.H.)

This single businessman in his early forties has been in therapy for six years. Narcissistic difficulties have prevented him from making a commitment to a long-term relationship. In other areas of his life obsessive-compulsive defenses help him function on a neurotic level. Expression of any emotion is difficult for him.

His first reference to the nuclear issue was indirect. It occurred the week before the airing of the movie *The Day After*. Never having talked about political issues before, he spoke of admiring politicians for their capacity to be flexible. I noted that it was unusual for him to speak of politics and used the opportunity to ask if he planned to watch the film. He was initially surprised that I raised the subject of nuclear weapons. He experienced the question as my valuing, and having an interest in, his ideas. He discussed at length strong feelings about the politics involved, the absurdity of the mutual paranoia between the superpowers, and the fact that there are alternative ways to work out differences. He was surprised by the spontaneity and emotionality of his response, which I reinforced as positive. I encouraged his bringing up ideas about the arms race and/or politics in the future.

The hour after the movie he spent discussing his reactions. These comments were less cohesive, more intellectual, and manifested his underlying passive nature. The following week he mentioned the value of learning new ways to think about things and specifically referred to our discussion "of politics." He also said that he was in a despondent mood and did not know why. When I suggested that his mood might be related to the film he agreed that that was quite possible, saying that the Russians walking out of the recent arms-control talks did not help and that images from the movie had continued to stay with him.

He has talked about the arms race on one other occasion. He began the appointment immediately after the November 1984 elections by saying that he would like to be able to switch roles today and asked me how I felt about the elections. Though largely a projection of his own feelings, this expression of concern for my feelings involved a significant risk for him as revealing his own feelings directly makes him feel extremely vulnerable. I asked if he could first tell me his reactions. He had voted for the losing ticket and said he "has to hold on to the hope" that the people who surround the President are less radical and belligerent. He went on to say that he did not understand the personal greed that he felt was a major factor in the election. He then said that beyond voting there was nothing more he could do. I noted his usual passivity and spoke briefly of the many things people can and are doing. I then also answered his questions, saying that he accurately anticipated my disappointment and transient feelings of discouragement, but said that these were feelings I could bear without being overwhelmed, as he is learning to do. He was surprised to find we had spent the entire hour on the subject.

CASE 5 (I.J.)

This 40-year-old mother of two teenage children, and highly successful business woman, has been in intensive psychotherapy (five times a week) for two-and-a-half years. She had begun less intensive therapy one year earlier as her children's maturation and several major family-related crises had caused her previously intact narcissistic defenses to give way to severely incapacitating borderline pathology. She has required four hospitalizations during this time and has been in nearly constant turmoil. It is not surprising that there has been only one brief indirect reference to the arms race. This reference occurred the week before the showing of *The Day After*. In commenting about her general sensitivity to the suffering of others, she spoke of "even having difficulty seeing anyone suffer in movies or on television." I noted this comment and asked if she was planning to watch the film. She said that it was certainly something that her children had been talking about. Initially she said that she was going to watch. I reviewed with her the fact that such exposure to the nuclear issue can stir up very intense feelings for anyone and that it might be best for her not to watch it. She appreciated this recommendation and decided to avoid it. She changed her mind on the evening of the broadcast because she did not want to be isolated from her family. Interestingly, she in fact did not have any perceivable adverse reaction despite the fact that other programs dealing with violence or human suffering have been unbearably overwhelming for her.

CASE 6 (K.L.)

This single professional woman in her early thirties has been in weekly psychotherapy for five years secondary to difficulty entering a meaningful long-term relationship. She is neurotic with a hysterical personality organization. Her first reference to the nuclear issue was indirect. It involved concerns about her brother who she learned was a member of a survivalist group. After listening to her concerns about her brother, I noted that the existence of survivalist groups touched on the subject of nuclear weapons and asked if this was an issue she thought much about. She seemed mildly ill at ease with the topic. She said she did not think about it very much because she believed that the weapons would never be used: "Governmental officials would not be that irrational." She partially recognized the unrealistic nature of this perspective but said nothing more about it. As with my other patients, I indicated that it was a subject we could talk about in the future if she wanted to.

Shortly before the showing of *The Day After* she spontaneously spoke of anxieties about viewing the movie. Her orientation toward the movie and the issue was much more realistic than earlier. After the movie she recognized the danger of the situation and the necessity for people to become informed and active. She bought several books with this goal in mind.

A third reference occurred six months later. She had called and asked for an appointment earlier than our regularly scheduled time. As we walked to my office she commented on seeing an IPPNW flyer on the bulletin board and asked if I had put it up. I responded casually that I had not and that there were several doctors interested in the issue at the hospital. We spent the time reviewing a major interpersonal crisis that had erupted suddenly between herself and a housemate.

Several months later, in January 1985, when we were talking about her general problem with initiating involvements of any kind, she mentioned the books on the arms race as an example. She added, however, that she also had not been able to pick them up because the subject made her too anxious.

CASE 7 (M.N.)

The main psychological struggle for this single Jewish professional woman involves preoedipal separation anxiety related to her mother being a survivor of the Nazi holocaust. She has been in therapy for 9 years, progressing slowly from only once a week to three times a week.

Her first reference to the arms race occurred in June 1982, at the time she was making the pivotal career decision to leave graduate school without finishing her dissertation because of a need for the greater structure of a job. As she began her job hunt, she spoke angrily about the low salaries she would have to consider and said that she felt her line of work should be higher paid rather than having so much money channeled into building bombs. Given the intensity of her anxiety about this change, I chose not to note the comment and continued to focus on her immediate life concerns.

Eighteen months passed without further reference to nuclear issues. On the Monday after the airing of *The Day After* she was typically speaking of work-associated anxiety but not saying anything substantial. I decided to ask if she had watched the movie. She had not, but proceeded with a detailed description of how she perpetually attempted to avoid the subject. She said that in part this was because the arms race had a surrealistic quality to her in contrast to a more tangible issue such as world hunger. She also felt that her avoidance involved the word "holocaust," a subject relating to her mother's experience that she was not yet able to handle. She also said that she frankly felt that the issue would be too overwhelming for her. I supported these efforts, noting that they involved knowing her limitations and that it was acceptable for her not to feel she personally must take on responsibility for it.

This discussion did not have a discernible adverse effect. A few weeks later she spontaneously said that our discussion of the arms race had in fact been helpful. She felt less guilty about her difficulty exploring her feelings about the holocaust. She had experienced my sanctioning her avoidance of the arms race as generally saying that she does not "have to" spend so much time worrying about social injustices, past or present.

The subject came up two more times, both in March of 1984. There were no particularly significant life events occurring during this time. During an hour that involved a discussion of why she felt a desperate need to be in "control," she spoke of an underlying fear of things giving way inside her, "like quicksand." She associated to her childhood thoughts about her mother and to the imminent sense that "it" (the holocaust) could happen again. She spontaneously noted that this is why she avoids discussion of the arms race. I discussed this childhood fear that the world is a terribly dangerous place and how this fear derived from inconsistent parenting (in part patterned by her mother's unresolved post-traumatic syndrome). I told her that despite the arms race the world is not as dangerous as she believes, particularly the events of her day-to-day life that continue to evoke unwarranted anxiety. Two weeks later she mentioned the arms race again, saying that working on an issue like that would be more fulfilling than her job. I noted, in contrast to her earlier fears, that she now seemed able to refer to nuclear weapons without intense anxiety. She indicated that my helping her overcome her guilt about not being involved had made a real difference.

CASE 8 (O.P.)

A single Japanese-American professional women in her late twenties was referred to me for a moderately severe panic disorder. (The referring doctor did not know the patient's ethnic background and O.P. had no possible way of knowing of my disarmament work.) She has been in once-a-week therapy now for one year. Her first and only explicit reference to nuclear weapons occurred during our third hour. Both because of the early stage of treatment and my sense that this issue would prove to have profound significance in this young woman's intrapsychic life, I chose not to note her initial comment. It occurred as she briefly described her parents. They had met and married in Japan shortly after World War II. Her Japanese mother, I learned subsequently, was within twenty miles of Hiroshima, had to be relocated briefly after the bombing, and had contracted tuberculosis shortly after the war ended. The patient's father was a career noncommissioned military man. In describing him, the patient said, "He is a real Archie Bunker type, very aggressive. You know, drop the bomb, a World War III type."

Ten months later, after discussing the significance of childhood experiences, I gave her some literature that dealt with the mental health issues of Japanese Americans. I mentioned that it unfortunately did not discuss World War II wives or their families and commented on the heterogeneity of "minority" groups. She said, "Like the Jewish people." The spontaneity of this comment and the reference to Jews seemed more than coincidental to me. I noted this and shared with her my impression that she had something in common with Jewish people in the sense that she is the child of a survivor of the Japanese holocaust. I then noted that she had made reference to nuclear weapons when she first described her father. She accepted these comments with interest. Not having been an introspective person, not involved with politics, she said that she had not thought much about the arms race or the personal significance of her mother's experience.

CASE 9 (Q.R.)

A 20-year-old patient began intensive psychotherapy when referred for longer-term hospital treatment for a recurrent psychotic illness. I learned shortly into our work that she listened to the album *Pink Floyd the Wall*. I told her I was familiar with the album and how it involved a person going crazy. Because trust was a major therapeutic concern, I did note the nuclear theme that is central to the album.

The patient was discharged after six months and continues three-times-a-week therapy. She had been doing quite well until her home burned down while I was on vacation. She barely escaped the fire. An increase in medication had helped her sleep, though nightmares involving the fire occurred nightly. This crisis had prompted her to be uncharacteristically open the first two weeks after I returned. During the third week she reported being more "spacey" (racing, incoherent thoughts) over the weekend. During our second appointment that week, evidence of paranoid psychotic ideation was present and included the sense that I knew about those who were watching her. Her more healthy self was sufficiently intact so that by the end of the hour she was not convinced of these beliefs.

During the next hour she was more cohesive. The troubling thoughts had diminished in their intensity. She mentioned early in the hour liking a song that deals with the Viet Nam War. She then quite spontaneously shared with me that for a number of years she had waves of fear of the world being destroyed by nuclear war. She said that it was not something that was currently affecting her, though it was clearly related to the recent catastrophe in her life. I told her that it was something we could talk about. I asked if she recognized this theme in *Pink Floyd the Wall*. She said that she did but generally listened to it because she identified with the protagonist's psychotic decompensation. She also said that she was not aware of my involvement in disarmament work. We spent no more than 10 minutes on this subject and went on to plans for her weekend. Her clinical state did continue to deteriorate and she required hospitalization a week later.

CASE 10 (S.T.)

A 13-year-old son of an arsonist and wife-beater flopped on the chair at his 14th hour. He mentioned that the rabbi had talked again about the Holocaust in Hebrew school. He was mad at the rabbi for returning to European Jewry: "The next holocaust will make us all glow in the dark, and we have no control over that, so it makes no sense to remember," he said. The exploration of nuclear fears allowed us to talk about his overwhelming fear and anger about his past and his bleak vision of his own future.

CASE 11 (U.V.)

A 20-year-old Jewish woman had been abused sexually for nine years by a family friend. During the first year of therapy she talked about her admiration of Nazis, SS uniforms, Panzer divisions, and so forth. In the second year of psychotherapy she spoke about her confusion over her role in the abuse, "like the bomb was dropped on me and I can't figure out who's responsible." She also felt intense hopelessness and fear not only about nuclear weapons but also about her failed attempt to control her sense of being abandoned to the bed of an abuser.

FOOTNOTES

(a) My clinical responses have been influenced by my involvement in disarmament work during this same period. I have given talks to the general public, facilitated small group discussions, provided consultation to the development of a conference on the potential role of mental health professionals vis-à-vis the arms race, worked on several committees of Physicians for Social Responsibility, and am currently providing consultation to a national disarmament organization. These activities have given me the opportunity to interact with hundreds of Americans at various stages of attempting to respond adaptively to the peril of nuclear developments.

REFERENCES

1. Sylvia Plath, "Mary's Song." In *Ariel*. N.Y.: Harper and Row, 1961.
2. Pink Floyd, *Pink Floyd the Wall*. CBS Records, 1979.
3. Kosta Tsipis, *Arsenal: Understanding Weapons in the Nuclear Age*. N.Y.: Simon and Schuster, 1983.
4. The Boston Study Group, *The Price of Defense: A New Strategy for Military Spending*. N.Y.: Times Books, 1979.
5. Robert C. Aldridge, *The Counterforce Syndrome: A Guide to U.S. Nuclear Weapons and Strategic Doctrine*. Washington, D.C.: Institute for Policy Studies, 1978.
6. Jonathan Schell, *The Fate of the Earth*. N.Y.: Knopf, 1982.
7. Richard P. Turco, O. Brian Toon, Thomas P. Ackerman, James B. Pollack and Carl Sagan, "Nuclear Winter: Global Consequences of Multiple Nuclear Explosions." In *Science, 222*, pp. 1283-1292.
8. Ruth Adams and Susan Cullen, eds., *The Final Epidemic: Physicians and Scientists on Nuclear War*. Chicago: Educational Foundation for Nuclear Science, 1981.
9. Robert Scheer, *With Enough Shovels: Reagan, Bush and Nuclear War*. N.Y.: Random House, 1982.
10. Daniel Ellsberg, "First Strike: An Interview with Daniel Ellsberg." *Inquiry*, April 13, 1981, pp. 13-18.
11. Robert Scheer, "Fear of a U.S. First Strike Seen as Cause of Arms Race: Interview with McNamara." *Los Angeles Times*, April 8, 1982.
12. O. Eugene Baum, "Countertransference." *The Psychoanalytic Review*, Vol. 56, No. 4, 1970, pp. 621-637.
13. Group for the Advancement of Psychiatry. *Psychiatric Aspects of the Prevention of Nuclear War*, N.Y.: 1964.
14. Lester Grinspoon, "The Truth is Not Enough." In *International Conflict and Behavioral Science: The Craigville Papers edited by R. Fisher*. N.Y.: Basic Books, 1964.
15. Lester Grinspoon and E.J. Liebman, "Escape from the Bomb." *The New Republic*, Sept. 1961, pp. 10-15.
16. Robert Jay Lifton and Eric Elson, "The Human Meaning of Total Disaster: The Buffalo Creek Experience." *Psychiatry*, No. 3, 1976, pp. 1-9.
17. Robert Jay Lifton, *The Broken Connection*. N.Y.: Simon and Schuster, 1980.
18. Robert Jay Lifton and Richard Falk, *Indefensible Weapons: The Political and*

Psychological Case Against Nuclearism. N.Y.: Basic Books, 1982.
19. Jerome D. Frank, *Sanity and Survival: Psychological Aspects of War and Peace.* N.Y.: Vintage Books, 1967.
20. Group for the Advancement of Psychiatry.
21. Schell, *The Fate of the Earth.*
22. Erik H. Erikson, *Childhood and Society.* N.Y.: Norton, 1963.
23. Frank, *Sanity and Survival.*
24. Schell, *The Fate of the Earth.*
25. Lifton, *The Broken Connection.*
26. Erikson, *Childhood and Society.*
27. Lifton & Falk, *Indefensible Weapons.*
28. Schell, *The Fate of the Earth,* p. 97.
29. Michael Mufson, "Three Mile Island: Psychological Effects of a Nuclear Accident and Mass Media Coverage." *The Psychosocial Aspects of Nuclear Developments,* American Psychiatric Association Task Force Report, No. 20, 1982.
30. John E. Mack, "Resistance to Knowing in the Nuclear Age." *Harvard Education Review,* Vol. 54, No. 3, 1984, pp. 260-270.
31. Adela G. Wilkeson, "Nuclear Numbing and the Practice of Psychiatry." Presented at the 1984 American Psychiatric Association Annual Convention, available on audio cassette, Audio Transcripts Ltd., 610 Madison St., Alexandria, Va.
32. Roberta Snow and Eric Chivian, *There's a Nuclear War Going On Inside Me.* Educators for Social Responsibility Videotape, Cambridge, MA: 1983.
33. Eric Chivian and Roberta Snow, *What Soviet Children are Saying about Nuclear Weapons.* Educators for Social Responsibility Videotape, Cambridge, MA: 1984.
34. William Beardslee and John E. Mack, "The Impact on Children and Adolescents of Nuclear Developments." *The Psychosocial Aspects of Nuclear Developments,* American Psychiatric Association Task Force, No. 20, 1982.
35. Sibylle Escalona, "Growing Up with the Threat of Nuclear War: Some Indirect Effects on Personality Development." *American Journal of Orthopsychiatry,* Vol. 52, No. 4, 1982, pp. 600-607.
36. Delbert C. Miller, *Handbook of Research Design and Social Measurement.* N.Y.: McKay, 1970.
37. Pink Floyd, *Pink Floyd the Wall.*
38. T.S. Eliot, *The Cocktail Party.* N.Y.: Harcourt Brace Jovanovich, 1950, p. 132.

6

The Nuclear Bomb as a
Psychological Reality

Wolfgang Giegerich, Ph.D.

If we do not thoughtlessly repeat the phrase "The Nuclear Bomb As A Psychological Reality," but allow *what* it says to come home to us, then the bomb is somehow "impossible." The nuclear bomb and the soul seem to be almost contradictions.* The bomb on the one hand and psychological reality on the other may each independently be an acceptable topic, but the connecting "as" between them makes this title intolerable. Nevertheless, it is precisely this "as" which shall be our theme here. The at first undoubtedly disconcerting purpose of this paper is to contribute to the rescue of the nuclear bomb for the soul and to opening the soul for the nuclear bomb.

I begin with a sad fact: The nuclear bomb exists, and we are stuck with it. No matter whether disarmament negotiations will succeed or not, we will never be able to return from our knowledge of the bomb and our power to destroy the whole world back to a state of innocence, and therefore we can never be sure whether or not some crazy or evil person or state will sooner or later succumb to the temptation to put our

---

*The author uses the terms "soul" and "psyche" in this essay as defined by Jung; thus: "soul," a clearly demarcated functional complex that can best be described as "personality;" "psyche," "the totality of all psychic processes, conscious as well as unconscious" (Jung, C.G., *Psychological Types,* Bollingen Series XX, Princeton University Press, 1974, p. 463).—Editor's note.

knowledge of the bomb to use. So it is vital that the destructive potential be in some way defused, whereby it is of course not sufficient to defuse the actual bombs. Much more important would be to defuse our dangerous knowledge about the explosive potential of nature by somehow binding it, integrating it. For the trouble with defused or dismantled bombs is that they can at any time be re-fused and newly constructed, and thus we would always be in the most precarious situation of having to hope that man's soundness of reason, his goodwill and sense of moral responsibility will not break down.

It is relatively easy to defuse the bombs technically. But how to bind their destructive power in such a way that the existence of mankind is not dependent on the accidents and vicissitudes of our reasonable and peace-loving behavior is an unanswered question. There is one fundamental obstacle that makes it impossible for the time being to find an answer. This obstacle is that we live not in one reality, but in two separate ones. The nuclear bomb, for instance, is, to begin with, a physical, technical object for us. How to construct, repair, defuse or ignite it, how to finance it, where to position it and what diplomatic and strategic plans to formulate for its use—these questions are the domain of the technicians in the widest sense of the word, including economists, politicians, military men.

When psychologists, on the other hand, view the bomb, they deal solely with questions such as which repressed complexes made it possible in the first place to invent such an absolutely crazy thing as the bomb, which threatens not only the enemy, but us all. Or the questions of how to deal with our fears of the bomb and with our projected enemy imagos. The technical object thus may be caused by psychological factors in us, and may in return affect the soul by giving it nightmares, but it is not itself anything psychological. Only my fear of it is psychological, not the bomb itself. It remains outside of my inner reality as an external physical reality. So we can say that the psyche, the field of our human motivations, emotions, imaginings and behavior, has the bomb outside of itself as the bomb has the soul outside of itself.

This condition of a split of reality into two realities—one physical and technical and irrevocably non-psychological, one psychological and having the physical object irrevocably outside of itself—can itself be subjected to psychological reflection. It then appears as a most critical condition, as a split of consciousness, as a neurotic dissociation. In view of one and the same object, modern man has, as it were, two separate compartments at his disposal to organize his view of its reality as a whole. The one aspect of phenomena (the fears and hopes they cause, the moral obligation they impose on us and the like) is always placed in one compartment, and the other "external" aspect of the same phenomena into the other, so that the two aspects can never truly meet. To be sure, our world-view allows causal connections to run back and forth between the contents of the two compartments, but my fear of the nuclear bomb and the physical reality of this bomb nevertheless remain each in its own compartment.

Here you might immediately object that we can hardly speak of two compartments that *we* keep apart, but that there indeed exist two separate realities. It is a simple fact that fear is something internal, psychological, subjective in me, and the bomb something technical out there. To this I reply, surely, this is indeed true, but, and now comes the crucial point, it is only true for the Christian West, and even there only for the modern age. At no time before and in no other part of the world has reality been split apart in this manner. Not in China, not with the so-called Primitives, not in ancient Greece, to mention just three quite different examples. If the primitive looked at his carved fetish, it was not an exclusively man-made physical object for him that may have had certain effects on his soul, and, on the other hand, this effect was not a mere intrapsychic emotion. Rather, the real, "external" fetish was itself animated and alive. For the Greeks there was no juxtaposition of physics and psychology. Psychological phenomena such as love and anger belonged with all others in the one nature and were also subjects of physics, but physics not in the modern mathematical or even mechanistic sense, but in a "poetic" sense, precisely because soul and divine matters were a part of it.

Thus if we say that psyche and objective external world are indeed two separate realities, this does not mean that the separation is a fact of nature, but that it is a product of *history* and is subject to the conditions of the history of our soul. The historical relativity of this seemingly absolute truth must be made conscious by means of critical reflection. For us it is true that there are indeed two realities, because our consciousness has, long prior to our own thinking and perceiving, been split into those two compartments and because we, that is to say Western mankind, are residing within a neurosis. And perhaps there has only been this extreme technological development toward the nuclear bomb because technology has been split from the soul, and the soul, as the exclusively internal reality, had been split off from external reality so that the external world could undergo a development without any inherent restrictions or bondage.

As long as the two worlds are juxtaposed, we remain fundamentally threatened because all restrictions have to be imposed from outside, by us, by *our* morality and well-meaning. But such imposed restrictions will never be able to reach and affect the inner nature of the bomb and the explosive potential itself. The bomb, whether as factual object or as an idea, will remain untamed and there will remain a constant temptation to finally try it out, a temptation requiring tremendous efforts of the will to withstand. This most unsatisfactory condition can only be hoped to change if first the split dividing the psychological from the physical can be eliminated and if a state is reached in which the explosive nature outside is no longer cut off from the inner values, and the inner ethical and religious values are no longer split off from external reality. To allow us to understand this split more deeply and to move us a little closer to such a fusion of the psychological and the external is the purpose of the following reflections.

During the early Christian centuries, one tradition of thought held that woman did not have a soul. *Mulier non habet animam.* Nobody today would seriously deny woman's soul. We find this idea preposterous. And in fact, it is frequently thought today that if there is indeed a difference between the sexes regarding soul, then the greater affinity to soul must be ascribed to women, just as soulfulness tends to be understood rather as a feminine than a masculine quality.

But it would be a mistake to assume that because we think this way we had overcome the ancient tradition that declared woman devoid of soul. We overlook that we use the same thought pattern, with the only difference that there has been a shift from woman to external reality as a whole. Of course, we do not say, *woman* has no soul. But we say, external reality *non habet animam,* technology has no soul, technical objects are soulless. Only people have souls, only humans can be ensouled. The parallelism between the thesis, "woman has no soul," and the thesis, "the technical world has no soul," is not a merely accidental and formal one, but reveals a genuine connection. Both are an expression of the same stance, the same intellectual tradition. Both are informed by an archetypal fantasy, i.e., a pattern of thought that prior to any particular act of thinking and prior to any particular contents has long laid out the general course and structure that our thought must follow or comply with. The archetypal fantasy at work in the ideas at hand can be called "Manichean," in a loose sense. It is the vision of the world as being torn apart by a fundamental, inevitable opposition. On the one hand the "upper" world of spirit, of light and the good, on the other the "lower" totally corrupted, totally evil world of matter, of the body, the feminine.

This thought pattern still prevails undiminished today, even though it exerts its influence in a completely new shape. We no longer project the opposites onto the great mythical-metaphysical powers Spirit and Matter. Metaphysical ideas generally do not capture our imagination any more; they seem unreal and do not touch or move us, whereas there was a time when metaphysical differences even led to wars. Our thinking prefers "concrete" and "practical" problems. But this by no means implies that the metaphysical opposites Spirit and Matter have just disappeared. Today, they are simply immersed in the medium of the earthly or concrete. The place of Spirit and Matter is now taken by nature on the one hand and technology on the other. The "natural" is the present-day representative of what once was the principle of Spirit, for the natural is—no matter whether we are conscious of it or not—regarded as original purity, ultimately as God's unadulterated creation, pervaded by his spirit. Nature is, from the point of view of the objective psyche, no longer Mother Earth, female deity, mud and blood, giving birth and devouring. In truth, but in secret, it today has *logos* character and is of a spiritual nature, idea and ideal of the primal, the pure and true, the world before the Fall, as it was conceived in God's infinite intelligence. Nature had to have this quality ever since it was turned into the creation of the Christian God, who is absolute mind. Likewise, nature means a warm sentiment for the countryside and deep emotions at the sight of its grandeur for us, so it is regarded as soulful, for soul implies first of all feeling for modern man.

Technology (above all the nuclear bomb), by contrast, is that realm that in *our* time fulfills the other half of this archetypal pattern and must carry for us the stigma of the corrupted, evil world of matter, of the body, of darkness and of the feminine. After all, technology is what is responsible for the destruction of the environment and the rationalization of life, and the nuclear bomb in particular is thought of as the expression of our sin, as evil incorporated. Between nature and the invention of technology there is for our feeling a fundamental Fall.

Oddly, the archetypal fantasy of the corrupted world and the world of light today employs the idea of the opposition of the patriarchal and the matriarchal, of one-sided male rationality versus feminine values. Since this idea after all aims for a revaluation of the feminine, it looks at first glance as if all that was condemned in Manicheism—the lower fallen world of the body and the feminine—were freed here from this very condemnation, whereas the formerly upper world of one-sided male rationality were relativized and lowered. But today's popular contrast of the patriarchal and the matriarchal can easily be seen through as a new version of Manichean thinking—a new version which additionally has the advantage of being disguised as the opposite of itself, and thus can more easily be kept unconscious. For if we are *for* nature, for biologically grown food products, spontaneity, body work, and against the patriarchal, achievement-oriented mind-set, then this seems proof enough for our having renounced the Manichean emphasis on the pure realm of spirit and contempt for the earth.

But this is only what it looks like. For first of all it does not matter which of the two poles of the dualism is on top and which one below. It suffices that even if the contrast were turned upside down, the same dualistic *pattern* would still prevail, including the condemnation of the one pole and the praise for the other. Secondly, however, the dualism has not been turned upside down, but only renamed. Today as before, Spirit or Mind is what is good, and Matter is what is evil, the only difference being that unexpectedly Spirit is today to be found in the "unspoiled" world of the "primitives," in the "feminine" values of closeness to nature and spontaneity, of emotionality and body sensitivity, whereas the evil world of matter and of the feminine paradoxically takes on the trade name of the "patriarchal." For it is the "patriarchal" that gave rise to science and technology, and, as we said, technology is the guise in which the mythical idea of dark, feminine Matter is given to us today.

Technology is "materialistic," because according to general consensus it is materialistic and soulless to set one's heart on television sets, refrigerators, cars, computers and all the other technical gadgets. Technology is materialistic because as part of the capitalistic system with its advertising and its hunger for growth rates it serves the greed for profit and is under the charge of Mammon. But if it is materialistic, then it belongs archetypally to the realm of *mater,* the Great Mother, as much as it may empirically have been produced by men, may require rational thinking, and may lead to the rationalization of the production process in factories. The truly "matriarchal"—the world under the control of the Great Mother—simply is no longer the world of green earth, of plant growth, even if we still act as if it were, and the Great Mother herself is no longer the mistress of the animals (in a biological sense). She has long moved out of nature and of the bodily realm. Today the Great Mother rules in technology and over *economic* "growth." It is not without significance that factories and other industrial works are termed "plants," just as there is hardly a difference between the words "produce" for fruits and vegetables and "products" for what is manufactured in industries. The archetypal fantasy that prevails here and that informs us about the psychological place of the entire world of industry is evident: it is the sphere of the vegetation goddess, the mistress of the Earth.

That the sphere of technology is truly the modern form of the feminine, earthly, bodily, becomes fully apparent when we realize that it gets its full share of the Manichean condemnation of the body as the corrupted and evil. Just as woman once was blamed for the bodily existence and sensuousness projected upon her and was regarded as *vas iniquitatum,* vessel of sin, so technology is for us the source of a black substantiality and of an absolute evil: of pollutants, smog, poisonous waste, atomic rays and all kinds of contamination. These are the literal realization of black sin, which was once given only in the mode of a spiritual or mythical reality. It is as if the idea of corrupted matter could not rest until the absolutely harmful had factually and literally received an objective, concrete presence in our world so that the position of evil matter would be occupied by a visible and obvious symbol.

Of course, if generally in our age technology is ascribed to patriarchal thinking; if today the idea of the hypertrophic patriarchal and the dreadfully neglected matriarchal is common talk and arouses the feelings of the public, then one might on the basis of this general consensus assume that with this idea a simple truth must have been discovered. But for an archetypal, i.e., for a critical psychology, this looks very different. The fact that the cliché of the male-female or patriarchal-matriarchal contrast is that common and widespread is, from a psychological point of view, suspicious in itself. It gives the impression that an archetypal collective thought pattern, a mythical idea—the Manichean vision of the world that we have been talking about—has taken hold of consciousness and obscures the free, unprejudiced perception of the phenomena themselves. Our thinking is, so it seems, occupied and put into service by this mythical pattern so that we are compelled to measure all kinds of historical and present-day phenomena time and again with the same old yardstick and to take them prisoner for this modern myth of ours. It is important to be conscious of the power that this archetypal thought pattern has over us.

As so often, it takes the eye of the poet to see through the superficial aspect to the mythic image and by the same token to recognize in technology the *new* form of the feminine (in a mythic-psychological, not a biological sense!), to recognize that in the technical products the modern version of the anima has taken shape. I will present one example for this. The Flemish-French writer Huysmans has the hero of his 1884 novel *A Rebours* (*Against the Grain*) say that nature has been superseded and is in her dotage.

> Why, take the one of all her works which is held to be the most exquisite, the one of all her creations whose beauty is by general consent deemed the most original and most perfect,—woman to wit, have not men, by their own unsided effort, manufactured a living, yet artificial organism that is every whit her match from the point of view of plastic beauty? Does there exist in this world of ours a being, conceived in the joys of fornication and brought to birth amid the pangs of motherhood, the model, the type of which is more dazzlingly, more superbly beautiful than that of the two locomotives lately adopted for service on the Northern Railroad of France?
>
> One, the Crampton, an adorable blonde, shrill-voiced, slender-waisted, with her glittering corset of polished brass, her supple, catlike grace, a fair and fascinating blonde, the perfection of whose charms is almost terrifying when, stiffening her muscles of steel, pouring the sweat of steam down her hot flanks, she sets revolving the puissant circle of her

elegant wheels and darts forth a living thing at the head of the fast express or racing seaside special!

The other, the Engerth, a massively built, dark-browed brunette, of harsh, hoarse-toned utterance, with thick-set loins, panoplied in armour-plating of sheet iron, a giantess with dishevelled mane of black eddying smoke, with her six pairs of low, coupled wheels, what overwhelming power when shaking the very earth, she takes in tow, slowly, deliberately, the ponderous train of goods waggons.

Of a certainty, among women, frail, fair-skinned beauties or majestic, brown-locked charmers, no such consummate types of dainty slimness and of terrifying force are to be found...[1]

Huysmans does not merely perceive in technology the patriarchal and the rational. Nay, for his poetic and phenomenological eye technology is woman, wild beast, and he is far from disparaging this female, denying her soul according to the old motto, *mulier non habet animam,* or, according to the version prevalent today, "technology is soulless." Quite the contrary. What he presents is an image of the anima herself in two of her numerous possible shapes. Neither does he speak for or against technology; he merely shows its inner image, its psychological nature, i.e., how it appears if it is seen by the heart or by the soul and if our thinking is not caught in a disparaging myth.

This is not "merely" a "literary figure," a "metaphor," originating from "poetic license." It is a very strict observation accurately reflecting reality. The only difference from the customary external view of technology is that here it is seen from within, our glance penetrating to the psychological image. C.G. Jung also saw that there has indeed been a shift on the part of the anima from nature to technology.[2] He speaks of "channeling the religious numen into physical nature and ultimately into matter itself, which in its turn had the chance to become a self-subsistent 'metaphysical' principle."[3] I would say: to become the place and carrier of the objective psyche. Jung also points to a decisive change in unconscious symbolism: "Nowadays animals, dragons, and other living creatures are readily replaced in dreams by railways, locomotives, motorcycles, aeroplanes, and suchlike artificial products....This expresses the remoteness of the modern mind from nature; *animals have lost their numinosity;* they have become apparently harmless; instead we people the world with hooting, booming, clattering monsters....[4]

You may have heard of a psychotherapeutic method called sandplay, developed by Dora Kalff. In a sand tray of a certain size the patient in the analytic hour has to form a scene by shaping the sand in any way he pleases and by placing toy figures into it. He will not have been given a theme to create, but is told to follow the promptings of his imaginings and inner needs. In this way the most variegated sand pictures are produced. One person will perhaps fill the entire sand tray with water until only a small cone-shaped island rises above the surface. On this island he places a small boy. This picture might, for instance, display the psychological condition of an ego-consciousness threatened by the waves of the unconscious and barely capable of maintaining itself. Another person may construct a high wall down the middle of the sand tray, and to the right of this wall he meticulously levels the sand and places a few objects on it in geometric order, whereas to the left he creates a thoroughly chaotic situation. In this we might recognize an obvious self-manifestation of a neurotic dissociation, that is, of a psychological condition where there is no connection between the two poles of order and chaos, no give and take, but where both are absolutely separated from one another, here sheer chaos, there absolute order. These two examples are to give you at least a rough idea of the therapeutic sandplay.

I would like to use the idea of the sandplay as an analogy that is to help us to overcome that thought pattern which forces us to juxtapose the soul as the inner reality against an external reality conceived as soulless. I suggest that we try to look at the world of technical objects, of industry and of the economy as if they were a gigantic sandplay picture, a sand picture that has not been created by the individual scientists, technicians and industrial managers of history out of their personal inner needs, but one in which the collective unconscious or the objective psyche of Western mankind tried to express itself. The sand tray in which this sandplay takes place would not have the dimensions of 50 by 30 inches, and the figures to be introduced into the play would not be toy figures on a shelf. Rather, this would be a play in which the ''sand'' is the whole wide world and in which the figures are real, living people, we ourselves and mankind at large. All of modern history would then be, as it were, one single therapy session in which Western man has worked and is still working on the collective sand picture.

Correspondingly, one could see the worlds of other civilizations and other ages as their differing sand pictures. If, for instance, you look at the picture created by the primitives, then you find a social system of marriage classes with strict taboos and complex rules, you will find houses for the men's gatherings, masks and totem poles, bull-roarers, tatooing, animal sacrifices and what not. If you look at the sand picture of the Greeks, you find splendid temples, the poetry of Homer, the Greek Tragedy, the difference between free men and slaves, the institution of pederasty, the polis as the form of political unity, whereas, quite different again, the medieval sand picture is characterized by the division of power between emperor and pope, by knighthood, monasticism, trade guilds, by Gothic cathedrals and so forth. If however you look at our sand picture you find in it factories, conveyor belts, computers, paper-backs, quartz watches, nuclear bombs, social security, human rights and so on.

No sandplay, whether in psychotherapy or in history, can be called "wrong" as long as those playing do not betray the inner necessities of their picture, i.e., as long as they do not cheat. It is not "wrong" to depict the worlds of order and chaos in pure concentration and separated by a wall, even though it may be problematic or neurotic. The therapist could not be "against" such a picture and should not try to intervene and by way of setting things "right" advise the patient to tear down the wall separating the two realms. To the contrary, this picture is quite right and therapeutic in itself. For by creating such a sand picture the patient pro-duces for himself a visible vessel into which his whole soul, precisely with its split, can flow, a house into which the energies of his unconscious psyche can stream. Thus the split no longer remains locked in the im-prisonment of his own interior, but *presents* itself and creates for itself something real outside into which it can move and in which it can feel at home. This alone will get things moving in him.

The same applies to our collective sand picture too. In it, modern man has not built temples like the Greeks or cathedrals like in the Middle Ages—it is obvious that such would be inconceivable in the psychological situation of modernity. Rather, Western man's psychic energy flowed in-to the production of factories, machines, computers, weapons and also of the nuclear bomb. The scene depicted in this way is, to be sure, most dangerous, highly explosive, but this does not at all mean that this pic-ture, including the bomb, would be "wrong," as long as we are willing to look at it not only politically and morally, but truly psychologically. No, psychologically and therapeutically the nuclear bomb obviously is a cen-tral symbol of *our,* the modern, collective unconscious. With the bomb, the objective psyche tries to create for itself that visible vessel that would be capable of containing and holding the tremendous collective-psychological energies apparently unleashed in modern man.

Certainly, the nuclear bomb is a terrible threat, but it is also a con-tainer, a receptacle for the dangerous condition of the modern collective unconscious. And it would be unimaginable what would happen psychologically if we did not have at least this container, as insufficient as it may be, for the explosives in the collective psyche. For this dual im-age of threat and containing vessel, the bomb, is, just as C.G. Jung once said of the neurosis, "our best enemy or friend" and something eminent-ly therapeutic, perhaps even our only chance, for by mirroring our un-conscious, i.e., hidden condition, it alone can help us to an awareness of what tremendous energies must have been unleashed in the collective psyche and how charged the latter must be. Without the bomb we could continue for good to stay in our illusions and would not have to wake up to our reality. Just as the religious fervor of the Middle Ages demanded cathedrals so that there would be a vessel into which its psyche could flow, so too, it seems, does the unconscious psyche of modern man demand something like the nuclear bomb in order to have a visible equivalent and containment for a soul condition that is obviously highly explosive.

The sand picture of the psychotherapeutic session is an external, material reality, and yet it is not anything merely external. It is also, even primarily, something psychological. The medieval cathedral is a technical work, but nobody would think to say that it is nothing but a technical object. We all know that it is much rather something essentially religious and symbolic and the expression of the medieval soul. The same is true for the nuclear bomb. It is constructed by technicians, but this does not at all mean that it is something exclusively technical. Maybe it is only so difficult for us to see this because we do not see it from the distance of centuries as with the cathedral; secondly, because it is a terrible, not an inviting symbol; and thirdly, because it does not openly reveal its religious and symbolic character. In the case of the cathedral, the religious purpose is obvious and explicit. In the case of the bomb it is present just the same, but concealed. Like the cathedral it is *first* of an imaginal and psychological nature and only then also a technical object. It is a work of the poetry *(poïesis)* of the soul. The only difference is that our soul no longer flows into the beauty of Greek statues of gods or into the deep, intensive devotion of Gothic representations of the Virgin Mary, but it takes the shape of stylish cars, jets, moon rockets, of sophisticated microchips and radar screens, and instead of marble, bronze or oil paints, it makes use of glass fibers, nylon, silicon and uranium as its medium, in order to correspond to a fundamentally changed psychological reality.

Thus the world of technology does not have to be understood as a soulless external reality that at best is interacting with the psychological inner world. It could rather be a psychological phenomenon in its own right: the picture of the soul of modern man and his collective unconscious. The actual unconscious would then not only be *in* us, in man's interior, it would also be in our real world out there as it has been depicted in our "sandplay" in accordance with the inner needs and promptings of our soul. And the only question would be what attitude to take toward our soul picture, how to deal with it.

It can be that if we have created a sand picture or have had a dream we do not at all like the whole picture or one element of it. It could, for instance, be most embarrassing. In this situation there are several alternative ways of reacting. We can eliminate the embarrassing element from the picture or, in therapy, suppress the objectional dream scene when reporting the dream and act as if the picture or the dream were complete without this part. The disturbing half of the sand picture is declared as not belonging. Only the harmless right half of the picture, e.g., is now considered to be the actual picture. Of course this is cheating. We would just be fooling ourselves without changing the real situation in the least. But in the same manner one could also react to the bomb. Because it is so inhuman you could say, it does not belong to our sand picture. It is not the gloomy element in our picture that is just as much part of it as the light touches, but it is a mistake, an error in the construction of the picture. Our actual picture only includes the dignity of man, democratic freedom, prosperity and education for all, etc., but of course not poisonous waste, smog, nuclear bombs, slums and totalitarian regimes.

However, could it not be that the picture truly created by us is the *togetherness* of "love of thy neighbor" *and* the nuclear bomb, the togetherness of democratic freedom *and* armament, of humanism *and* exploitation, in other words that in this picture the nuclear bomb would be just as "right" as our humanism, and that the latter would only be true to the extent that the bomb is true too?

The philosopher Hegel said that truth lies in the whole, and this is correct at least in the case of a picture or a work of art. If *one* element, the nuclear bomb, is wished away from our sand picture, then inevitably all other elements too, indeed this picture as a whole, will no longer be true.

If in a picture you cannot have the desirable aspects without the painful ones and the latter not without the former, you might perhaps get the idea that it would be best to wipe out the entire sand picture and start all over again from scratch, creating a fundamentally new picture in which there is no need for an embarrassing or terrible element to begin with. But the perhaps much more harmonious second picture would not change the fact that the first picture was exactly as it was, including the embarrassing element. The psychological reality of the first picture is not really undone by wiping it out and creating a new one. It would only have become invisible to us, without, however, becoming any less real. We know this approach as utopian thinking, the wish for a total reform of society, for a return to nature or to any other new beginning, history to date in its entirety being condemned as a wrong development.

As a psychotherapist I am not happy with either possibility, for both amount to denial and repression. As a therapist, I do not have any knowledge about what a particular sand picture ought to look like. I rather try to see *how* it is and to work with what it actually contains, be it beautiful or ugly, delightful or terrible. The work of therapy can perhaps be best imagined in terms of the alchemical *opus*. Alchemy means work on the transformation of whatever substances are given. In this sense, what I mean is not a mere conservation or mending of an existing bad situation. It is certainly important that things change. But the question is how. If we follow alchemical thinking, everything that is part of our picture must be put into one alchemical vessel, as it were, so that the outrageousness of the nuclear bomb no longer remains *beside* our noble ideals such as human dignity, freedom of personal development and purity of the air, etc., but so that the outrageous and the noble touch each other, are cooked together and permeate one another. From this a new picture might originate, but this would not be, as in the case of utopian thinking, an absolute new beginning. It would be the same old picture, only in a new shape. All its ingredients would still be there, even those that the nuclear bomb is made of. It would be a transformation of the picture from within.

We cannot escape from the sand picture of our history, nor can we eliminate within our sand picture the terrible element. But it seems to me that the nuclear bomb is by no means itself the actual pathological problem. Much more pathological than the bomb is the splitting off of the idealistic half of our sand picture from the terrible half. In order to bring it down to a rather crude formula, the actual pathology consists in our keeping our humanitarian Christian consciousness and the nuclear bomb apart from each other in two separate compartments instead of letting them clash as the ingredients of one alchemical vessel, the components of our one mental reality, so that they could dissolve each other. What is more precarious is that we disown one aspect of the sand picture built by us as if it were an illegitimate child and disparage it as a bastard; in other words, we do not recognize it as *our* picture that makes the unconscious truth about ourselves visible for us. We are working at this picture, but then we contemptuously turn our backs on it and do not want to know about it, whereas it is the very purpose of sand pictures to tell us something about our hidden psychological condition, so that we can allow the new contents pushing to the fore from within the sand picture to become part of our conscious life.

That we disown our sand picture is revealed in our conceiving the nuclear bomb only as a technical external reality to which we have to react politically, morally and humanistically as to a literal armament and power problem. It shows in our refusing to also see it psychologically, i.e., as a soul image, as mythical figure and anima-like creature. This of course has the counter-productive result that our own attitude remains hardened by being fixated in the power complex and that technical reality will continue to remain deprived of the influx of heart and imagination that it so urgently needs. How are the external power structures materialized in the institutions of society and in objective realities such as armament to be lastingly softened if we ourselves meet them only with a power- and conflict-oriented frame of mind and deprive them of feeling qualities? But how can feeling, how can love flow into so-called external reality and animate it if we do not see the *image* hidden in it?

He who wants to have an expert understanding of the technical side of the nuclear bomb has to undergo a lengthy training in higher mathematics, in nuclear physics and engineering. But whoever wants to have his say in the matter of the psychological and moral aspect of the bomb seems to need only his conscience and a few categories like "good and evil," "patriarchal and matriarchal," "repressed aggressions" and "projection of enemy imagos." On the one, the technical side, the highest differentiation and professionalism, on the other, the psychological or ethical side, a cocktail party conversation level and a decided amateur status. Is it not frightening that such an extremely complex and sophisticated reality, in which the labor and ingenuity of centuries are invested, is met by such a simplistic frame of mind in us? It is as if we had a craftsman of the Middle Ages with his crude tools repair a computer, or a child be the pilot of an airplane. Something is obviously wrong here. The level of psychological and moral understanding surely should correspond to the level of differentiation reached in science and technology. The right to have a say in the psychological or moral evaluation of our situation would have to be acquired through just as differentiated a training in this area and by just as serious a concentration of the mind as is the right to a say in modern physics.

Why is this not the case? In this disconnection of the mental attitude from technical reality, the split of the one world into two realities (on the one hand objective nature studied by the sciences, and on the other hand our subjective attitudes and behavior studied in the fields of psychology and ethics) shows especially painfully. Because of this dissociation our consciousness can obstinately insist on staying at a naive medieval level and on approaching this absolutely incredible, unheard-of reality of the nuclear bomb with such ridiculously incommensurable categories as good and evil, war and peace, enemy imago and sorcerer's apprentice. Our consciousness can refuse to go along with the changes in the objective psyche, i.e., with the technological changes, and refuse to be truly affected and transformed by the fundamental explosion of all our traditional views and expectations during modernity. This is our main problem. The nuclear bomb by itself is comparatively harmless.

Can we really think that the challenge posed by the nuclear bomb can be met by our burdening *reality* with the task of adapting to the ideals of our ego? Or is it not we, today's mankind, who have to step by step adapt to the unheard-of situation out there by summoning all our strength and faculties and by sacrificing long-cherished moral and religious ideas, as painful as this may be?

What is this unheard-of situation necessitating our transformation into a fundamentally new human condition? It is that the objective psyche has long emigrated from the macrophysical world of things perceivable with our unarmed senses, and has settled on the level of nuclear particles and subcellular biology. The world as we have known it has fallen apart into its nuclear particles. Its very foundations have cracked. The natural world has once and for all become obsolete; it now has only the same degree of reality that a facade has. Today the real world *is* as it is shown to us by nuclear physics. The chairs on which you are sitting are not what they seem to be: solid matter. For the most part they are empty space, hardly interspersed with minute particles in cosmic distances from each other. We know this, but we do not admit it. Our consciousness wants to cling to the medieval mode of perceiving the world as consisting of formed things, bodies. It is deaf to the message of its own scientific knowledge, and succeeds in pretending to be deaf by declaring the results of science as belonging to one compartment, that of the material external world which allegedly has nothing to do with our subjective experiencing, our feelings, views and values, in short with the psyche. Indeed, we feel that our well-meaning consciousness must militantly defend the old views and values as an inner possession against the objective facts established by science. But the results of science do have to do with our psyche. We belong to this change as to our sand picture, to our hidden truth. This change is such a fundamental event in the history of the soul that it must no longer be kept from our consciousness. All our faculties must concentrate on slowly bringing our mode of existence more and more into correspondence with the sand picture which has long been before our eyes, but has been rejected and denied by us, its builders. This is the task of the future. And on our mastering this task will also depend whether we will be able or not to do justice to the main symbol of the new nuclear level of reality: the nuclear bomb.

REFERENCES

1.   Joris-Karl Huysmans, *Against the Grain,* with an Introduction by Havelock Ellis. N.Y.: Illustrated Editions Company, 1931, p. 104f. I am indebted to James Hillman who kindly pointed out this passage to me.
2.   Wolfgang Giegerich, "Das Begräbnis der Seele in die technische Zivilisation," *Eranos,* Vol. 52, 1983.
3.   C.G. Jung, *Mysterium Coniunctionis.* Vol. 14 of *The Collected Works of C.G. Jung.* 2nd Edition; edited by Herbert Read, Michael Fordham, Gerhard Adler, Willaim McGuire. Princeton, N.J.: Princeton University Press, 1974, p. 127.
4.   C.G. Jung, *Letters.* Vol. 2. Edited by Gerhard Adler & Aniel Jaffé, Princeton, N.J.: Princeton University Press, 1975, pp. xlvi-xlvii.

7

Human Disconnection and the Murder of the Earth

Deborah Rinzler, Ph.D.

Our appalling capacity as human beings to inflict damage, death and torture upon other people, animals, trees and plants, and natural systems in general has its roots in a profound and terrifying disconnectedness from ourselves as physical organisms. We live among and depend upon other physical organisms in the vast, complex, and beautiful environment of the earth, but this is not important to us at all. We are tragically unaware, on a daily, minute-to-minute basis, of the physical processes within us that keep us alive, that nurture us, renew us, equilibrate us, protect us. We display a callous and grandiose ingratitude toward the millions of microscopic organisms that make up what we call "my body," which function collectively, cooperatively, and with breathtaking efficiency, to get us from here to there. And it is even worse than ingratitude: the devaluing of our physical selves and our worship of mind, logic, rules-to-live-by, precepts, and other intellectual constructs have removed us so far from the wholesome interconnectedness of the living and non-living beings of the earth that we are truly on the brink of irreversible catastrophe: world suicide.

I do not think it is too great a leap to say that the abuses we have

*This chapter originally appeared, in somewhat different form, in the *Journal of Transactional Analysis,* October 1984.

forced upon our planet—the pollution of her water, air, and soil; the grouting-out of her insides for ore and nuclear fuel; rerouting her rivers; "improving" her coastline, and all the rest—is a direct consequence of our disconnection with our sensory, physical selves. If we do not feel ourselves as whole organisms, for which the alteration, removal, or "improvement" by artificial means of any part of us is a traumatic blow to the whole of us, we surely cannot feel the earth as a whole in which nuclear blasts in the South Pacific deposit clouds of radioactivity in the Eastern United States. Our personal rejection of our own sensations affects the entire earth.

As a psychotherapist, I have had abundant experience of well-meaning, intelligent, and largely emotionally-intact people tell me that their sensations "don't count." It is often not important to them that their physical experiences clearly indicate their need to cry, stretch, eat, fast, hit, throw up. These simple, basic sensory realities are regarded as entirely irrelevant to a mysterious process they call "finding the answers," "deciding what to do," "achieving my goals." My clients are not, as a rule, especially driven, ambitious, or heartless people. They have simply been conditioned to believe that the solutions to problems in living must and should be found in the realm of thought and logic. We have all been trained to disregard simple, sensory clues about our being—the very clues which, if accepted, acknowledged and honored, would place us squarely on the path of a more wholesome, integrated, connected way of life.

If I have been conditioned to believe, as many of us have, that anger is a bad thing, I have learned to hate my anger. I have learned to hate and reject *the sensations of my anger,* whatever they may be for me: I will hate and reject my heart beating faster, my blood flowing to my hands and feet, the feeling of increased adrenalin, the desire to open my throat, to yell. And whenever I feel those sensations, I will hate and reject myself for having them. The whole natural physical response and process of "being angry," no matter what the cause, has become a threat to me, a part of me I must expunge. And while I may *know,* intellectually, that there is nothing inherently wrong with being angry, I cannot accept anger in myself until I have learned to tolerate my physical sensations of anger when they occur. To tolerate these sensations means that I must permit myself to experience these sensations for as long as they last, without attempting to stop them, without saying, "This is bad; this should not be happening; I shouldn't be feeling this; I don't want to feel this." My refusal to feel or to tolerate my sensations because they are "bad" is as absurd as would be my refusal to accept the falling of a waterfall, its sound in my ears, the spray on my face. The waterfall *is:* my anger *is.* My anger, my sensations of anger, do not threaten me *until* I make the judgment: "I should not be feeling this.'"

I may also reject my anger by saying, "It does not matter that I feel this." And so, I will not attend to the cue of my anger to defend myself, to communicate honestly with a friend, to feel the right to violate a rule I know to be unjust. Rather than accepting responsibility for my anger, I simply discount it.

If I can say that it does not matter that I feel sensations of anger, I can also say that it does not matter if I feel the spray of a waterfall. The devaluing of any particular sensation or set of sensations generalizes rapidly to the devaluation of them all; first my anger, then a waterfall and all waterfalls are made irrelevant by my attitude. The waterfall might as well be submerged in concrete to build a new airport, or a high-rise, or another suburb.

Similarly, if I have been conditioned to believe that crying is a sign of "weakness," it is then necessary for me to reject in myself any sensations which I associate with crying: tightness in my chest, constriction in my throat, a feeling of fullness behind my eyes. I will struggle to pretend that these sensations are not happening to me, and eventually perhaps deaden myself to them so I literally do not know any more what I am feeling. Or, I will feel these crying sensations, and harden myself against them in a conscious, self-critical struggle not to cry, creating chronic and unnatural muscular defensiveness in the process. There are many combinations and variations on this theme of self-rejection, and especially when the sensations of crying are concerned, this rejection is dangerous. If I cannot let myself cry, feel hurt and pain, I also cannot be moved by a symphony, by the fear of a child, by the slow death of a planet. If I cannot permit myself to feel soft and vulnerable for myself, how can I have any empathy or softness for anyone, anything, else?

Our daily disconnection from our sensations causes us to abuse ourselves physically. Overeating, overdrinking, compulsive exercise, underexercise, fad and crash diets, compulsive overwork, all result from our having inadequate experience of what we are and what we need on the organismic, sensory level. Either we actually do not feel our sensations—many people with whom I have worked are at first truly unaware of having sensations—or we feel sensations which we then deliberately, whether consciously or not, judge, deny, interpret and devalue. Then, we try to *think* what we should do to feel better, to "live right," to "be in shape." There are habitual runners, for instance, who feel they have done something morally wrong if, because they have injured a foot, pulled a muscle, whatever, they do not run for a day. The runner acknowledges the sensation of physical pain sufficiently so that he does not run, but the reason for not running, being "only physical," is not enough. He must feel guilty for not running. A man I know told me recently that he went to work with a bad flu, a fever of 102 degrees, and many symptoms of being very ill, because it was "stupid" to feel that way. "Just" sensations, "just" the physical messages, are unimportant.

And so: we are fragmented, dislocated from our bodily selves, living a life located unnaturally in the intellect. When we pay no attention to sensation, life feels strangely quiet and insubstantial; we feel like empty, brittle shells. Far from the natural sources of our being, far from a reverent contemplation and experience of our natural processes—our breathing, our movements, the sounds we hear and the sights we see, our sense of being *alive*—we seek sensation from outside ourselves, having forgotten that sensation lives within us. We seek drugs, lots of sex, loud music, entertainment in many forms, wishing to be filled with sensation. First we deny and reject our own life source; then we scramble to get some sensory nourishment from an ersatz source.

Certainly we are capable of being responsive on the sensory level to external stimulation all the time. At any moment, at this moment, we can become aware of things outside our physical selves acting on our eyes, ears, skin. But somehow we do not realize that the feeling generated is *inside* us, *is* us. The impoverishment of our experience is enormous.

Lacking this sensory knowing, this sensory experience of ourselves, devaluing and perpetually in conflict with many of the quiet, wordless, simple sensations that inform us at every moment of the complexity and wholeness of our being, we hide in our thoughts, our images, our self-images. We *fear* our sensations, paradoxically, as threatening to our being. We fear and reject an entire level of our functioning, of our lives, of ourselves. And if we fear and reject ourselves, how can we have compassion for ourselves?

If we do not have compassion for ourselves, we cannot have compassion for the real and natural things that surround us: people, animals, trees, grass, earth, water, air. The destructiveness we perpetrate on the Earth is the inevitable extension of our own personal rejection and abuse of our physical selves. And unless we each learn to connect with, accept, acknowledge, and honor our own sensations, and live harmoniously with them, we will not learn to honor the organism of the earth, its rhythms and processes, its creatures and foibles. And if we cannot sense the truth, we will die.

We do not only lack compassion for the sensations of our own living organisms—ourselves—and for the organism Earth—a lack of compassion taught to us from very early in our lives by parents and teachers who had no compassion for *them*selves. We also display an appalling *hubris* or arrogance toward our sensations: arrogance about the moment-to-moment cues or clues about our physical existence on the level of our individual bodies, and, by inevitable extension, toward the sensory movements, processes, and interactions of the natural world in which we are embedded. Thus: if we arrogantly ignore the sensory messages that clearly are instructing us that we need to cry, we may easily ignore with similar arrogance the sensory messages and requirements of the earth. If it is not important, because we arrogantly and arbitrarily decide that it is not, to permit our tears to flow, then we will arrogantly build dams to stop the flow of rivers, backing up the water to form artificial lakes, flooding natural valleys with water that never belonged there, drowning entire ecosystems, from algae and mosses to raccoons, rabbits, and deer. If we work ourselves far past healthy physical limits by saying it is "stupid" to be sick, by ignoring our sensory symptoms that we need rest and nourishment, we will also ignore the symptoms of the sickness of the earth, her dying and extinct species, her vanishing forests, her eroding soil, her tainted water, her thick and granular air. We seem to have no connection with the natural needs of the earth to be left alone. If I do not, cannot, must not, let myself cry, what difference is it to me if I reroute the Colorado River?

When we are numb to our own physical messages, we become numb to our own genuine suffering. Our indifference to and arrogance about our sensory selves creates a consciousness which regards it as natural, ordinary, and a matter of course to kill house mice with spring traps and poison (the mice are our enemies, like the sensations we reject), shoot deer for sport and ride home with their carcasses sprawled on top of our cars, bulldoze flowering trees to build parking lots. Perhaps at times we must take measures to intervene, to interfere with natural systems, but what is alarming is that we do these things so blithely, so easily, so unfeelingly, without pain or hesitation, without a thought or hope that another solution could be found, without sorrow or compassion for the harm or disruption or torture inflicted. Why not choose mousetraps which allow us to relocate, rather than kill, the mice? Because we do not regard a mouse as a feeling creature, as a being that *matters,* whose existence and subsequent non-existence has an impact on the world as a whole. And this can only be because we ourselves feel we do not matter, do not fit, have no impact—no more impact than the pricking of tears behind the eyes that we fight down and ignore.

We feel and act *as if* we are in fact disconnected, physically, spiritually, ecologically, and morally, from ourselves and from the universe. We behave *as if* we were each isolated and separate. We cut ourselves off from the roots and springs of life within us—our sensations—and therefore from each other and from all else that is. Inevitably, this leaves us lonely, and it leaves us enraged: enraged because we do not permit ourselves to have within our life experience the richness that belongs to us. Feeling raped, deprived, and "empty" (this peculiar word comes up often in my sessions with clients, and almost always turns out to refer to the person's unawareness of sensation), we make awkward, ineffectual, and often aggressive attempts to connect with ourselves and with others. We embark on rigorous programs of exercise, pushing ourselves past our pain and fatigue, just to feel some sensation. We take drugs which change our experience of ourselves in a confused attempt to feel something other than what we are already feeling. And we start fights: become provocative, pushy, controlling, manipulative, in a sad charade of actual connection, actual contact, because we do not understand, do not *feel,* that we are already connected.

The seventh-century mystic Avva Dorotheus imagined human connection as a great wheel or sun with many radiating spokes or rays; we are each on one of the rays, and as we each approach the center, we are more and more closely connected to each other, and, in Avva's conception, to God. I like to conceive also that all the beings of the universe, living and non-living, are with us on this wheel. We may all approach the center as closely as we can, or as we will let ourselves, but nowhere on the wheel, even on the periphery, are we ever *not* connected with the center and with the whole. One of Buddha's basic teachings was that all the world's creatures are connected, and that the pain and suffering of one affects the whole: the whole wheel.

We have detached ourselves from knowing that we are all on this wheel, already connected to everyone, everything, on it, and this causes us to be tragically unaware of, detached from, the pain and suffering of other human beings. In order to maintain this awareness, we must be aware of ourselves, and this we do not do. Although we know, intellectually, of the horrors suffered by the people of Hiroshima and Nagasaki, we do not connect. We see movies or photographs of these people walking along like moving corpses, skin scorched and peeling off in sheets, bleeding, eyes melted by the blast and the heat and the flash of the bombs. We keep these images, and the sensations they evoke, within our awareness for a time, and then thrust them out. And so, due to our unawareness, we now have enough nuclear bombs for thousands and thousands of Hiroshimas and Nagasakis—for billions of charred and roasted corpses with melted eyes. If we had remained aware of these sensations and images, we could not have permitted, could not now permit, more bombs to be built. But we are unaware.

At this writing, it appears clear that at least the voting majority of adults in the United States regularly denies the evidence of its senses. The poverty that we see; the increased and increasing prices of all the things we buy; the daily stories of murder on every scale, from individual homicide to civil wars in Lebanon and Central America; the commonplace and hideous violations of human rights in this country and most others, are available to our eyes, ears, and sensibilities in general. And yet, it seems possible for this voting population to deny this evidence utterly, and instead to grasp the less grounded and rooted images of an Administration which doggedly denies these sensory realities, and offers as an alternative comforting words astoundingly bereft of concrete meaning: "There is no hunger in this country," "The United States has returned to its former glory," "We can prevail in a nuclear war."

This final chilling statement by Secretary of State Caspar Weinberger (but it could have been almost anyone in the present Administration), so tragically and appallingly removed from the facts, is truly the result of what can only be called a dangerous and mentally unhealthy disconnection from and denial of physical reality. In actuality, of course, nuclear war on any scale would range—has already begun to range—from the slow death of the organism Earth from increased incidence of cancers, genetic damage of all species, and ecological disruption due to virtually irreversible radioactive pollution, to its rapid and cataclysmic end in nuclear holocaust. *We have already had abundant sensory evidence* of the hideous damage nuclear technology has done to us and our home.[1], [2], [3], [4] And to the extent that we deny this evidence, we increase the probability of our mass suicide and the murder of the earth.

But our words and thoughts have become at times entirely disconnected from their roots in our sensations, our experiences, and so we must grab these essentially contentless, bloodless, and meaningless verbalizations to guide us in our actions and to dictate our futures, for want of more reliable data. For instance, certain jobs are enormously stressful, with high incidence of stress-related disease: flight-control positions; certain executive jobs; many subordinate roles such as those filled by secretaries and flight attendants; control personnel in nuclear power stations. We who work at these jobs simply *don't feel well.* We have the opportunity every day of our lives to attend to our physical selves, to feel the muscle tension, digestive upset, headaches, whatever, that we *know* are generated by our work and working conditions. But our logic, our words, tell us something contradictory: "This is my livelihood; I have been trained to do this, so I should like it; it would be impractical financially to change jobs; I am climbing this corporate ladder, so I have to stay here," and so forth. And we ignore the concrete sensory signs that we are growing every day more ill, more damaged, and because we have these words to guide us in a direction in which we *think* we must go, we make no move, either to find work that is consonant with organismic health, or to change the conditions of our present work situations so they are less stressful, more nourishing of our whole being.

Our overbalanced reliance on ultimately hollow words, thoughts, and logic, at the expense of our compassion for the suffering of our physical selves, creates in us a chronic state of passivity and victimization. Any anger we feel at our victimization we must also reject; it is not "logical." When we forego the evidence of our senses, we give anyone, anything, outside us the power and the authority to step in and tell us what is good *for* us—our parents, teachers, political leaders, government agencies, the

TV set. And everyone's words will suffice to convince us that they all know what we need, as long as we are told what we want to hear. This is why thousands of us in this country live without protest in the vicinity of nuclear power plants. We are told: this is safe; this technology is advanced and cannot go wrong; this small amount of radioactive gas released from here will not harm you and your children; you are going to be just fine; "Go play in the nuclear power park."[5] And we wait, and wait, with an underlying sense of anxiety to which we are told not to attend; we are told that there will not, cannot, be a disaster, a meltdown, an explosion, and that anyway if there is—in itself a massive contradiction we are also taught to ignore—safely following the evacuation plans will save us. Before the near-meltdown at Three Mile Island in Harrisburg, Pa., it was perhaps not as clear that we felt this inner fear of nuclear power plants, but now we *see* what can happen. The people around TMI suffered and continue to suffer from that accident. They are depressed, tense, anxious,[6] more reliant than before the accident on tranquilizers, alcohol, and cigarettes,[7] and afraid to have babies for fear of genetic damage from the radiation released during the accident.[8] They live in daily anticipation of developing cancer; some already have cancer.[9] Will those of us living near other nuclear power plants *see* these victims? *Hear* what they are saying? *Feel* their pain, their fear, their outrage? Will we *listen* to our own sensations of dis-ease living near our Indian Point, our Browns Ferry, our Pilgrim? Or will we deny these sensations, and passively wait, hearing only the reassurances of the "authorities," telling us we are perfectly safe? Are we going to reject what we *know,* and become another group of nuclear victims, of victims in general?

We are also told that, in spite of our pervasive and entirely realistic fear of nuclear war, of annihilation, of mass suicide, we should not be afraid of nuclear weapons. Nuclear weapons are good for us, we are told; they keep us safe; they protect us. And in spite of what we know, there are many of us who *want* to hear this, to be told that everything is all right. We seek inappropriately for safety and protection in the shelter of governmental rhetoric, when the only safety and protection we can ever know is in our profound connectedness with our sensory selves, as part of the living earth, warning us of our danger. But our fatal passivity, our eager willingness to believe that mere words, stripped of all feeling connection to the concrete reality of sensory experience, will keep us safe, have permitted some of us to produce the most bizarre verbalizations, the most deplorable actions, actions so split off, so disconnected from the health and wholeness of our planet, and of our selves, that their results are suicidal. For instance, Secretary of State Henry Stimson, on May 16, 1945, less than three months before the United States government experimented with atomic weapons on the populations of Hiroshima and Nagaski, stated that "precision bombing" in Japan was important because "the reputation of the United States for fair play and humanitarianism is the world's biggest asset for peace in the coming decades."[10]

Likewise, William Lawrence, the science-writer/chronicler of the beginning years of this country's experiments in nuclear technology, and who watched many atomic tests, wrote:

> For nearly an hour after the fireball had faded I watched incredulously the great many-colored cloud that had been born in a gigantic pillar of fire. This cloud rose and spread until the boiling mushroom at its top had reached about twenty-five miles into the atmosphere and covered a stretch of sky, now tinged by the rising sun to the east of it, about a hundred miles long.
>
> Having seen what a much smaller fireball and mushroom-topped cloud had done to the city of Nagasaki, I was momentarily staggered by the thought of what the fireball and mushroom I was then watching would do to any of the world's great cities—New York, Washington, Chicago, Paris, London, Rome or Moscow. But then, as I kept on watching, a second, more reassuring thought became uppermost in my mind, a thought that has kept growing ever more reassuring in the years that have followed....
>
> This great iridescent cloud and its mushroom top, I found myself thinking as I watched, is actually a protective umbrella that will forever shield mankind everywhere against threat of annihilation in any atomic war....
>
> This world-covering, protective umbrella...will continue shielding us everywhere until the time comes...when mankind will be able to beat atomic swords into ploughshares...[11]

There is such total splitting off from physical reality, such disconnection from concrete sensation, in these verbalizations, that it seems to me they can only be called the results of psychotic thought processes. And yet, this way of thinking is rampant in our country, and in our world. We have become a race of psychotics, living according to the rhetoric of the moment, cut off from the life within us, murderous to ourselves and others. And so it goes, in our bizarre fashion: we are so disconnected from our natural, organic processes of growth and change that we actually believe, to the extent that we repeatedly and doggedly translate the belief into action, that we can *force* other people, other governments, to behave in a manner that we call more humane and compassionate. We actually have faith that murder, covert operations of the CIA (or KGB), military interventions on the ground, sea, and air, and ultimately the threat of using nuclear weapons, will make people be nice to each other: be democratic; be communists; be religious and god-fearing; be moral; be kind.

How is it possible to use the methods of coercion, torture, and brutality to teach harmony, morality, and compassion? To display our "humanitarianism"? How is it possible to use a first-strike nuclear weapon, the MX missile, to keep the peace? How is it possible to pretend that this is genuine compassion, genuine peace-seeking? And how is it possible, once we have seen this hollowness, this psychosis, to do nothing to stop it?

There is an unexamined assumption in all of this mad, destructive behavior in the name of peace, the assumption that we should, because it is our right, impose our view of the world, our need for our image of our security, on everybody else. If I wish to see myself as peaceloving and humanitarian, and insist that everyone else should be like me, I will first deny and reject my murderous *sensations* (i.e., my anger), and then feel free to behave in a murderous fashion (to drop nuclear bombs, for instance) as long as I call my behavior some word that is consonant with my image of myself. I beat my child not because I *feel angry,* but for her own good; I will destroy entire civilizations not because I am a murderer inside, but because it is for the good of humanity to be securely dead rather than insecurely Communist.

On a smaller scale, many psychotherapists, for instance, are taught to view the people they call "patients" through the eyes of whatever psychological theorist or theorists they have studied. Psychotherapists are seldom taught to be aware of their own and their clients' sensations, of the concrete bits and pieces of both their sensory life experience which would enable them truly to know themselves and each other. The result of this unbalanced training is that the therapist will superimpose a theoretical viewpoint on her client's reality like a mask, blinding them both to the workings of the client's inner life and preventing any real interactive connection between them. If I am busy seeing you, thinking about you, as a bundle of neurotic, oedipal, defensive structures, I will not sense that you are afraid, lonely, trembling, tense, excited, creative.

If I cannot sense that you are afraid, that you are creative—if I cannot sense your actuality, your reality in this moment—surely I will not sense or know that the people of El Salvador and Nicaragua have their own needs for their own government and not for one I insist they should have. Surely I cannot have respect, admiration, and compassion for the inner life and culture of the Russian people, for their history of suffering, for the terrible economic, social, and spiritual crisis they are experiencing today. I cannot see *any* people if all I am seeing are "Communists." Because of my need to maintain and protect my self-image, my theory, the way I want to see myself, I reject sensations of who I actually *am* at any given moment; and I reject *you*. I live in fear of what we both *are* in entirety, and seek "security" in means that will kill us both, kill us all.

What, after all, is this elusive state we call "security?" As Robert Lifton points out, security really means "safety or freedom from danger or risk. More specifically it refers to 'feeling no care or apprehension' (the word secure being derived from the Latin sè [without] cùra [care]."[8] But upon careful examination, we will realize that what we seek is not security at all, but stasis. We want everything to be always the same: our image of ourselves, our national image, our feelings, our sensations. We want to feel "happy." We do not want to feel anything new, anything different from before. We are truly conservative: nothing should change, everything should always be the same as it always was. Seeking "security," or rather stasis, in a perpetually changing world of flow and process, we live paradoxically in terror of change. Living in terror of process and change, we are profoundly out of place. Seeking to stop flow and process to prevent change, we also prevent growth and freedom. Preventing growth and freedom, we make ourselves dead: dead to ourselves, dead to the process of life. And the *sine qua non* of all the ways to prevent process, growth and life is to build, store, and use nuclear weapons. Nuclear weapons are the protectors of stasis, "national security," and death. Their very existence is the guardian of stagnation and the enemy of harmony and organic change.

Our apparent control of nature, as tragically opposed to our connection with nature, is a deep but paradoxically reversible fatal malaise. Our human malaise of disconnection from natural sensation, our symptoms of violence on all levels, our lack of compassion for our home the Earth, our incomprehension of the connectedness among all the things of the Earth, of the universe, are curable—if we are willing. If we are willing, each of us individually, to re-embrace the sensory richness that is ours to have, to accept, honor, and acknowledge ourselves as sensory organisms that change and grow, if we are willing to give up our worship of words, thoughts, and logic and learn also to value our physical selves, then perhaps there is hope. We must also be willing to connect with mice and mosquitoes, rivers and waterfalls, trees and grass, not for our own edification, use, and enjoyment, but simply for their existence which is as valuable as our own. It is clear that if we do not do these things, we are going to die, and we may die soon—of global pollution, of destruction of the Earth's resources, of impoverishment of the gene pool through extinction of species, of nuclear holocaust: of human arrogance. Unless we begin, each one of us, to connect with what is real and sensory and living within us, we will die. Would it be possible for us to begin today?

REFERENCES

1. Harvey Wasserman and Norman Solomon, *Killing Our Own.* N.Y.: Delta, 1982.
2. Alice Stewart, et al., "A Survey of Childhood Malignancies." *British Medical Journal,* 1958, pp. 1495-1508.
3. Ernest J. Sternglass, "Cancer: Relation of Prenatal Radiation to Development of Disease in Childhood." *Science,* June 7, 1963.
4. Rosalie Bertell, "Radiation Exposure and Human Species Survival." *Issue Papers: Working Documents of 10 March 1980 Public Meeting,* Vol. 1. Bethesda, Maryland: Committee on Federal Research into the Biological Effects of Ionizing Radiation, National Institute of Health, 1980.
5. John W. Gofman and Arthur R. Tamplin, *Poisoned Power.* Emmaus, Pa.: Rodale Press, 1971.
6. Robert Holt, Ph.D., New York University Psychologist, April 1980 interview quoted in Wasserman and Solomon, *Killing Our Own.*
7. Pennsylvania Department of Health, *Health Department Releases TMI Stress Study.* Harrisburg: Department of Health, April 17, 1980.
8. Kari Light, R.N., Representative, People Against Nuclear Energy (PANE), Middleton, Pa. Report given at public conference, "Nuclear Realities: From Victim to Activist," October 22, 1983.
9. *Ibid.*
10. Henry Stimson, Memo to President Truman, May 16, 1945, as quoted in Robert Jay Lifton, *The Broken Connection.* N.Y.: Touchstone, p. 378.
11. William L. Lawrence, *Men and Atoms.* N.Y.: Simon and Schuster, p. 197.
12. Robert Jay Lifton, *The Broken Connection.* N.Y.: Touchstone, p. 352.

8

Buddhist Resources for Moving Through Nuclear Death

Joanna Macy, Ph.D.

To live in the nuclear age is to live on the brink of time. The arms race and the destruction of the environment, together with the spread of conflict and oppression—these developments render questionable the very survival of the human species. They summon us urgently to collective action if disaster is to be averted. Yet, while customary forms of educational and social action appear more necessary than ever, they are also by themselves inadequate. For the dangers confronting us, and the horrors they portend, are of such magnitude as to numb the human psyche, building resistance to the very information we most need to convey and to face.

To overcome this numbness and resistance, a new dimension of social action has emerged, one which is essentially psychological in nature. Spreading through writings, conferences and workshops, it is known by a variety of names: "despair-work," "despair and empowerment work," "interhelp," or simply the "inner" work of social change. It expands awareness of both the peril and promise of our time, by first tapping our existential responses to the current crises. It "reframes" these responses and offers ways of transforming them into courage, compassion and commitment to act.

To date an estimated 100,000 people in the U.S., Canada, United Kingdom, Germany, Holland, Sweden, Norway, Japan, Australia and New Zealand have participated in these workshops; and a growing number of psychotherapists, as well as pastoral and school counselors, have incorporated the approach and methods of this work into their practice. The work is undertaken predominantly, but not exclusively, as a group process or experience, and is most effective when that experience is ongoing in the context of one's local community or organizational life. While it has engendered many articles, the most complete description to date is offered in my book *Despair and Personal Power in the Nuclear Age.*[1]

To an extent that the book does not elucidate, Buddhist teachings have been intrinsic to the genesis of this work. Other resources are important, too; in developing despair-work, I drew on general systems theory, humanistic psychology, and my own religious roots in the Judeo-Christian heritage. Indeed, I can and often do present the work solely in terms of one or the other of these Western tributaries. But more crucial to my development of the work have been my own Buddhist practice, my doctoral studies in Buddhism and systems theory, and my years of experience with the Sarvodaya Shramadana Movement, a Buddhist-inspired village self-help movement in Sri Lanka. While not necessarily evident to the many who engage in it, and while the effectiveness of the work in no way depends on an acknowledgment of these roots, Buddhist teachings have been integral to its unfolding.

The Buddhist sources of despair-work are twofold. One is doctrinal or conceptual, through the interrelated teachings of *dukkha* (suffering), *anicca* (impermanence), *anatta* (no self) and *paticca samuppada* (dependent arising). The other is methodological or practical, through the adaptation of Buddhist meditations. Let us see how the teachings function in helping people to break through denial and psychic numbing, and to transform the experience of pain for our world.

I
Philosophical Premises

Dukkha (Suffering)

"Suffering is." It constitutes the First Noble Truth and one of the three marks of existence. The Buddha began not with prescriptions, theories, revelations or comfort, but empirically with the existential fact of human pain, especially psychological pain. To find our way through the confusion and distress of our time, that is where we begin, too. That is what we know most immediately and incontrovertibly.

At the outset of the workshops, participants are usually invited to share a recent incident or piece of information which caused them pain for our world. In the safe setting which the group provides, these experiences surface quickly—a child's nuclear nightmare, the pollution of a nearby river, reports of war or starvation or expiring species of animal life. As participants hear themselves and each other give voice to their social despair, it ceases to appear as a personal morbidity or an idiosyncratic aberration. Its validity and universality become apparent. And because this pain arises from a level deeper than opinions and partisan allegiances, it undercuts our tendency to engage in debate. Argument often serves as an avoidance mechanism, when we are faced with frightening information; but when the focus is on our feeling response, argument is irrelevant; what emerges is the commonality of our caring. Shared pain for the world becomes the ground on which we rediscover our capacity for compassion and mutual trust.

Anicca (Impermanence)

One of the reasons we repress despair is the fear that, if we let ourselves experience it, we will become "stuck" or mired in it. In despair-work, however, as in insight meditation, we experience that "all dharmas are anicca": all phenomena, thoughts and feelings are transient. It is only our denial of them that lends permanence to our feelings, and freezes us in relation to our pain for the world. Once brought into the light of conscious awareness, the impacted pain begins to loosen and flow. It holds less terror for us when we experience its dynamic quality, its ebb and flow, as we cease holding it at arm's length and let it pass through us. As our resistance against it dissolves, we open to wider currents of knowing—currents of connection and caring.

Anatta (No Self)

Our inner responses to the world's distress are also blocked by fear that we might fall apart. Prospects of global disaster and knowledge of present destruction and suffering seem too overwhelming for the separate ego to cope with.

If we *are* but separate, self-existent egos, our pain for the world is hard to credit; there is no reason why we should be experiencing it. If all our drives and desires are essentially motivated by individual needs for pleasure and power, whence come our tears for our fellow-beings, for those unseen and those yet to be born? Are we sick? Neurotic? Traditional mainstream Western psychology, being largely ego-based, tends to reduce such distress to private pathology, seeking its cause in personal history and personal maladjustment. This tendency, of course, encourages the repression of despair, and increases the sense of isolation and craziness we can feel when it breaks through our defenses.

In despair-work, the sharing and validation of our pain for the world—of our co-suffering with it—give the lie to such reductionism. In the process it reveals that our experiencing does not arise from an isolable, autonomous self so much as from our interaction with the world around us. As we sense the truth of that, experiencing how ever-flowing perceptions, feelings and knowings interweave us into the wider fabric of existence, we cease to fear that we will fall apart. Our defenses and comforts may shatter, but the self is not an object that can break.

Such inklings are close to the Buddha's teaching of *anatta* or no self. Just as the illusion of separate selfhood is seen in the Dharma as a chief obstacle to enlightenment, so also, in the context of despair-work, it constitutes a hindrance to our capacity to deal with our feelings of planetary anguish. When we move beyond that illusion, shedding the need to protect a fragile self from painful information, we move beyond denial, avoidance and numbness as well. The reverse is equally true: the acceptance of our pain for the world validates our interconnectedness and loosens the bars of egocentricity.

Paticca Samuppada (Dependent Co-arising)

The Buddha's central doctrine of dependent co-arising (paticca samuppada) presents us with a view of reality where all is interconnected and interpenetrating—self and other, thought and deed, mind and form. From such a perspective the military, social and environmental dangers that threaten us in this planet-time come from no source external to the human psyche: they are reflections of it. They mirror its fears, greeds and hostilities, just as the psyche itself is conditioned by the institutional structures in which we live. Self and society are interdependent. This understanding is very close to the systems view that emerges from contemporary science, and also to the holographic model of the universe, in which the whole is reflected in each of its parts.

Despair-work is posited on a similar premise or intuition: that each of us, indissolubly and inextricably interconnected with the vaster web of life, is ultimately inseparable from the fate and experience of other beings. In our time of crisis this mutual belonging is perhaps most manifest in our inchoate feelings of pain for the world—of suffering on behalf of the whole.

In the workshops, as participants share this kind of suffering, it is valorized as an appropriate and wholesome response to current conditions and, furthermore, named and seen as proof of our interconnectedness. Breaking out of the isolation in which many have harbored their feelings, participants "come home" to their intrinsic mutuality. The sense of home-coming is so vivid that the response is often one of joy, even hilarity. Feelings of pain for the world are not purged thereby—nor can they be, for each day's news brings fresh signals of distress—but they are taken henceforth as reminders and proof of our interexistence, which in turn serves as a source for resilience and creative action.

To express this wider, interdependent sense of being, a number of images tend spontaneously to emerge in the course of the work. Participants speak of being as interrelated as the cells in a body, or as neurons in a neural net. Such images are appropriate to the synergy experienced in despair-work. Synergy ("power with"), like the power of neural interactions, springs from openness and responsiveness (response-ability), in contrast to the old hierarchical notion of "power-over," which is identified with armor, defenses and invulnerability. The recurrent image of neural network is very close to that of Hua Yen Buddhism. There, in the Jeweled Net of Indra, all beings are seen as nodes in a limitless web; each reflects all the others and, at each node too, intelligence and compassion can co-arise entire.

II

Practical Grounding

Conditioned to conceive of ourselves as separate, competitive entities, we need help to sustain the sense of interconnectedness and the synergistic power it can give us for social action. Here again, Buddhist teachings have been useful. Certain meditational practices, adopted and adapted in the course of despair-work, provide this assistance. Initially offered and rehearsed as guided meditations to groups, they can serve as an ongoing personal discipline, geared for use in daily activities and encounters. As such, they remind us that we do not need to withdraw from the world in solitary prayer or meditation, or even espouse a religious faith, in order to begin to wake up to the power and freedom innate in the human psyche.

To illustrate, here are four meditations that I frequently offer in the course of despair and empowerment workshops. These four exercises are on death, compassion, mutual power and mutual recognition. While they happen to be adapted from Buddhist teachings, they belong to us all as part of our planetary heritage. No belief system is necessary, only a readiness to attend to the immediacy of one's own experiencing. They will be most useful if read slowly with a quiet mind (a few deep breaths help), and if put directly into practice in the presence of others.

Meditation on Death

Most spiritual paths begin with the recognition of the transiency of human life. Medieval Christians honored this in the mystery play of *Everyman*. Don Juan, the Yaqui sorcerer, taught that the enlightened warrior walks with death at his shoulder. To confront and accept the inevitability of our dying releases us from attachments, frees us to live boldly, alert and appreciative.

An initial meditation on the Buddhist path involves reflection on the two-fold fact that: "death is certain" and "the time of death, uncertain." In our world today, the thermonuclear bomb, serving in a sense as a spiritual teacher, does that meditation for us, for we all know now that we can die together at any moment, without warning. When we deliberately let the reality of that possibility surface in our consciousness, it can be painful, of course, but it also helps us rediscover some fundamental truths about life. It jolts us awake to life's vividness, its miraculous quality as something given unearned, heightening our awareness of its beauty and the uniqueness of each object, each being.

As an occasional practice in daily life:

> Look at the person you encounter (stranger or friend). Let the realization arise in you that this person may die in a nuclear war. Keep breathing. Observe that face, unique, vulnerable...those eyes still can see; they are not empty sockets...the skin is still intact...Become aware of your desire, as it arises, that this person be spared such suffering and horror, feel the strength of that desire...keep breathing...Let the possibility arise in your consciousness that this may be the person you happen to be with when you die...that face the last you see...that hand the last you touch...it might reach out to help you then, to comfort, to give water. Open to the feelings for this person that surface in you with the awareness of this possibility. Open to the levels of caring and connection it reveals in you.

Breathing Through (Fostering Compassion)

Our time assails us with painful information about threats to our future and the present suffering of our fellow beings. We hear and read of famine, torture, poisonous wastes, the arms race, animals and plants dying off. Out of self-protection, we all put up some degree of resistance to this information; there is fear that it might overwhelm us if we let it in, that we might shatter under its impact or be mired in despair. Many of us block our awareness of the pain of our world because our culture has conditioned us to expect instant solutions: "I don't think about nuclear war (or acid rain) because there is nothing I can do about it." With the value our society places on optimism, our contemplation of such fearful problems can cause us to feel isolated, and even a bit crazy. So we tend to close them out—and thereby go numb.

Clearly, the distressing data must be dealt with if we are to respond and survive. But how to do this without falling apart? In my own struggle with despair, it seemed at first that I must either block out the terrible information or be shattered by it. I wondered if there was not a third alternative to going numb or going crazy. The practice of "breathing through" helped me find it.

Basic to most spiritual traditions, as well as to the systems view of the world, is the recognition that we are not separate, isolated entities, but integral and organic parts of the vast web of life. As such, we are like neurons in a neural net, through which flow currents of awareness of what is happening to us, as a species and as a planet. In that context, the pain we feel for our world is a living testimony to our interconnectedness with it. If we deny this pain, we become like blocked and atrophied neurons, deprived of life's flow and weakening the larger body in which we take being. But if we let it move through us, we affirm our belonging; our collective awareness increases. We can open to the pain of the world in confidence that it can neither shatter nor isolate us, for we are not objects that can break. We are resilient patterns within a vaster web of knowing.

Because we have been conditioned to view ourselves as separate, competitive and therefore fragile entities, it takes practice to relearn this kind of resilience. A good way to begin is by practicing simple openness, as in the exercise of "breathing through," adapted from an ancient Buddhist meditation for the development of compassion.

> Relax. Center on your breathing...visualize your breath as a stream flowing up through your nose, down through windpipe, lungs. Take it down through your lungs and, picturing a hole in the bottom of your heart, visualize the breath-stream passing through your heart and out through that hole to reconnect with the larger web of life around you. Let the breath-stream, as it passes through you, appear as one loop within that vast web, connecting you with it...keep breathing...
>
> Now open your awareness to the suffering that is present in the world. Drop for now all defenses and open to your knowledge of that suffering. Let it come as concretely as you can...concrete images of your fellow beings in pain and need, in fear and isolation, in prisons, hospitals, tenements, hunger camps...no need to strain for these images, they are present to you by virtue of our interexistence. Relax and just let them surface, breathe them in...the vast and countless hardships of our fellow humans, and of our animal brothers and sisters as well, as they swim the seas and fly the air of this ailing planet. Breathe in that pain like a dark stream, up through your nose, down through your trachea, lungs and heart, and out again

into the world net...you are asked to do nothing for now, but let is pass through your heart...keep breathing...be sure that stream flows through and out again; don't hang onto the pain...surrender it for now to the healing resources of life's vast web...

With Shantideva, the Buddhist saint, we can say, "Let all sorrows ripen in me." We help them ripen by passing them through our hearts...making good rich compost out of all that grief...so we can learn from it, enhancing our larger, collective knowing...

If you experience an ache in the chest, a pressure within the rib case, that is all right. The heart that breaks open can contain the whole universe. Your heart is that large. Trust it. Keep breathing.

This guided meditation serves to introduce the process of breathing through, which, once experienced, becomes useful in daily life in the many situations that confront us with painful information. By breathing through the bad news, rather than bracing ourselves against it, we can let it strengthen our sense of belonging in the larger web of being. It helps us remain alert and open, whether reading the newspaper, receiving criticism, or simply being present to a person who suffers.

For activists working for peace and justice, and those dealing most directly with the griefs of our time, the practice helps prevent burnout. Reminding us of the collective nature of both our problems and our power, it offers a healing measure of humility. It can also save us from self-righteousness. For when we can take in our world's pain, accepting it as the price of our caring, we can let it inform our acts without needing to inflict it as a punishment on others who are, at the moment, less involved.

The Great Ball of Merit

Compassion, which is grief in the grief of others, is but one side of the coin. The other side is joy in the joy of others—which in Buddhism is called *muditha*. To the extent that we allow ourselves to identify with the sufferings of other beings, we can identify with their strengths as well. This is very important for our own sense of adequacy and resilience, because we face a time of great challenge that demands of us more commitment, endurance and courage than we can ever dredge up out of our individual supply. We can learn to draw on the other neurons in the net, and to view them, in a grateful and celebrative fashion, as so much "money in the bank."

The concept here resembles the Christian notion of grace. Recognizing our own limitations, we cease to rely solely on individual strength and open up to the power that is beyond us and can flow through us. The Buddhist "Ball of Merit" is useful in helping us see that this power or grace is not dependent upon belief in God, but operates as well through our fellow beings.

In so doing, it lets us connect with each other more fully and appreciatively than we usually do. It is most helpful to those of us who have been socialized in a competitive society, based on a win-lose notion of power. "The more you have, the less I have." Conditioned by that patriarchal paradigm of power, we can fall prey to the stupidity of viewing the strengths or good fortune of others as a sign of our own inadequacy or deprivation. The Great Ball of Merit is a healthy corrective to envy. It brings us home, with a vast sense of ease, to our capacity for mutual enjoyment.

The practice takes two forms. The one closer to the ancient Buddhist meditation is this:

> Relax and close your eyes, relax into your breathing. Open your awareness to the fellow beings who share with you this planet-time...in this room...this neighborhood...this town...open to all those in this country...and in other lands...let your awareness encompass all beings living now in your world. Opening now to all time as well, let your awareness encompass all beings who ever lived...of all races and creeds and walks of life, rich, poor, kings and beggars, saints and sinners...like successive mountain ranges, the vast vistas of these fellow beings present themselves to your mind's eye...Now open yourself to the knowledge that in each of these innumerable lives some act of merit was performed. No matter how stunted or deprived the life, there was a gesture of generosity, a gift of love, an act of valor or self-sacrifice...on the battlefield or workplace, hospital or home...from each of these beings in their endless multitudes arose actions of courage, kindness, of teaching and healing. Let yourself see these manifold and immeasurable acts of merit...as they arise in the vistas of your inner eye, sweep them together...sweep them into a pile in front of you...use your hands...pile them up...pile them into a heap...pat them into a ball. It is the Great Ball of Merit...hold it and weight it in your hands...rejoice in it, knowing that no act of goodness is ever lost. It remains ever and always a present resource...a resource for the transformation of life...and now, with jubilation and gratitude, you turn that great ball...turn it over...over...into the healing of our world.

As we can learn from modern science and picture in the holographic model of reality, our lives interpenetrate. In the fluid tapestry of space-time, there is at root no distinction between self and other. The acts and intentions of others are like seeds that can germinate and bear fruit through our own lives, as we take them into awareness and dedicate, or "turn over," that awareness to our empowerment. Thoreau, Gandhi, Martin Luther King, Dorothy Day, and the nameless heroes and heroines of our own day, all can be part of our Ball of Merit, on which we can draw for inspiration and endurance. Other traditions feature notions similar to this, such as the "cloud of witnesses" of which St. Paul spoke, or the Treasury of Merit in the Catholic Church.

The second, more workaday, version of the Ball of Merit meditation helps us open to the powers of others. It is in direct contrast to the commonly accepted, patriarchal notion of power as something personally owned and exerted over others. The exercise prepares us to view them with fresh openness and curiosity as to how they can enhance our Ball of Merit. We can play this inner game with someone opposite us on the bus or across the bargaining table. It is especially useful when dealing with a person with whom we may be in conflict.

> What does this person add to my Great Ball of Merit? What gifts of intellect can enrich our common store? What reserves of stubborn endurance can she or he offer? What flights of fancy or powers of love lurk behind those eyes? What kindness or courage hides in those lips, what healing in those hands?
>
> Then, as with the breathing-through exercise, we open ourselves to the presence of these strengths, inhaling our awareness of them. As our awareness grows, we experience our gratitude for them and our capacity to enhance and partake...

Often we let our perceptions of the powers of others make us feel inadequate. Alongside an eloquent colleague, we can feel inarticulate; in the presence of an athlete we can feel weak and clumsy. In the process, we can come to resent both ourselves and the other person. In the light of the Great Ball of Merit, however, the gifts and good fortunes of others appear not as judgments, put-downs or competing challenges, but as resources we can honor and take pleasure in. We can learn to play detective, spying out treasures for the enhancement of life from even the unlikeliest material. Like air and sun and water, they form part of our common good.

In addition to releasing us from the mental cramp of envy, this spiritual practice—or game—offers two other rewards. One is pleasure in our own acuity, as our merit-detecting ability improves. The second is the response of others, who—while totally ignorant of the game we are playing—sense something in our manner that invites them to move more openly into the person they can be.

Learning to See Each Other

This exercise is derived from the Buddhist practice of the Brahmaviharas; it is also known as the Four Abodes of the Buddha, which are lovingkindness, compassion, joy in the joy of others, and equanimity. Adapted for use in a social context, it helps us to see each other more truly and experience the depths of our interconnections.

In workshops, I offer this as a guided meditation, with participants sitting in pairs facing each other. At its close, I encourage them to proceed to use it, or any portion they like, as they go about the business of their daily lives. It is an excellent antidote to boredom, when our eye falls on another person, say on the subway. It charges that idle movement with beauty and discovery. It also is useful when dealing with people whom we are tempted to dislike or disregard; it breaks open our accustomed ways of viewing them. When used like this, as a meditation-in-action, one does not, of course, gaze long and deeply into the other's eyes, as in the guided exercise. A seemingly casual glance is enough.

The guided, group form goes like this:

> Sit in pairs. Face each other. Stay silent. Take a couple of deep breaths, centering yourself and exhaling tension. Look into each other's eyes. If you feel discomfort or an urge to laugh or look away, just note that embarrassment with patience and gentleness toward yourself and come back, when you can, to your partner's eyes. You may never see this person again; the opportunity to behold the uniqueness of this particular human being is given to you now.
>
> As you look into this being's eyes, let yourself become aware of the powers that are there...open yourself to awareness of the gifts and strengths and the potentialities in this being...Behind those eyes are unmeasured reserves of ingenuity and endurance, wit and wisdom. There are gifts there, of which this person her/himself is unaware. Consider what these untapped powers can do for the healing of our planet and the relishing of our common life...As you consider that, let yourself become aware of your desire that this person be free from fear. Let yourself experience how much you want this being to be free from anger...and free from greed...and free from sorrow...and the causes of suffering. Know that

what you are now experiencing is the great lovingkindness. It is good for building a world.

Now, as you look into those eyes, let yourself become aware of the pain that is there. There are sorrows accumulated in that life's journey...There are failures and losses, griefs and disappointments beyond the telling. Let yourself open to them, open to that pain...to hurts that this person may never have shared with another being. What you are now experiencing is the great compassion. It is good for the healing of our world.

As you look into those eyes, open to the thought of how good it would be to make common cause...consider how ready you might be to work together...to take risks in a joint venture...imagine the zest of that, the excitement and laughter of engaging together on a common project...acting boldly and trusting each other. As you open to that possibility, what you open to is the great wealth; the pleasure in each other's powers, the joy in each other's joy.

Lastly, let your awareness drop, deep within you like a stone, sinking below the level of what words or acts can express...breathe deeply and quietly...open your consciousness to the deep web of relationship that underlies and interweaves all experience, all knowing. It is the web of life in which you have taken being and in which you are supported...Out of that vast web you cannot fall...no stupidity or failure, no personal inadequacy, can ever sever you from that living web. For that is what you are...and what has brought you into being...feel the assurance of that knowledge. Feel the great peace...rest in it. Out of that great peace, we can venture everything. We can trust. We can act.

I offer a practice that is corollary to the earlier death meditation, where we recognize that the person we meet may die in a nuclear war. Look at the next person you see. It may be lover, child, co-worker, postman, or your own face in the mirror. Regard him or her with the recognition that:

This person before me may be instrumental in saving us from nuclear war. In this person are gifts for the healing of our planet. In him/her are powers that can redound to the joy of all beings.

In concluding this chapter, let me say that it has been gratifying to acknowledge the debt that this work owes to Buddhist psychology, philosophy and practice. Yet it is also my belief and my experience that other major religious traditions, as well as the systems perspective of modern science, offer guidance in moving through the dark of our time and in finding, through the acknowledgment and sharing of our pain for the world, the power to redeem it. It is perhaps the distinctive gift of the Buddha that the insights and methods he offered are so universally applicable. Refusing to be drawn into debates on the correctness of differing views and opinions, he focused, like a physician, on one fact above all—that there is suffering. Because his teachings pre-eminently and empirically address that fact, they remain relevant and can nourish other traditions, other societies.

REFERENCE

1.   Joanna Macy, *Despair and Personal Power in the Nuclear Age.* Philadelphia: New Society Press, 1983.

9

Beyond Private Practice:
An Approach to Mental Health
in the Nuclear Age

Chellis Glendinning, Ph.D.

I was a psychotherapist in private practice from 1973 to 1980, but a development in 1979 led me to close my practice. This development was not a shift in my approach necessitating further training. It was not doubt about the effectiveness of psychotherapy, or even a job offer in a new field. It was Three Mile Island. This paper concerns the impact of that event on my thinking about the role of individual clinical practice in relation to a global mental health issue. It concerns working with people in large and small groups to attempt to heal the psychic wounds inflicted by the advent of nuclear technology and the arms race, and it is about one particular group process I have used for that purpose.

Anatomy of a Nuclear Age Ritual

That week as the nuclear power station in Pennsylvania teetered on the edge of meltdown, I, residing 2000 miles away in San Francisco, experienced the intensity of feeling I might were the plant in my own neighborhood. By day I darted from radio to newspaper to television, consuming every word of every report as if my life depended on it. At night I lay half-asleep/half-awake feeling myself hanging from the slenderest of threads, dangling in space with no support, no Mommy, no Daddy, no help.

*The author wishes to thank Harris Peck, M.D., for his help in preparing this chapter.

I endured that week alone. In those days the topic of the danger of nuclear technology was taboo, and to speak of it—even as a nuclear power plant neared meltdown—was denied. Because of my acquaintance with psychological process, though, I was able to steer my own course. I scrupulously acknowledged each feeling that bubbled up inside me. Fear. Anger. Despair. Grief. Surrender. Urgency. As I did, I became aware that just as emotional patterns we manifest in adult life mirror mechanisms developed at an earlier age, so these feelings harkened back to an earlier era. For the first time in almost 20 years, I was experiencing a sense of universally impending danger. This time its catalyst was an industrial accident, but the long repressed material—laced with memories of grade-school bomb drills, the day the Russians exploded an H-bomb, and the Cuban Missile Crisis—was the threat of nuclear war.

At this point I made a number of realizations. First of all, the techno-historical forces we face—from blatant nuclear technologies to the more insidious environmental contaminators—have as potent an impact on our human psyches as do our families and early education. This idea was a personal revelation, but it has since been documented by a number of researchers including Robert Lifton,[1] William Beardslee and John Mack,[2] and Benina Gould.[3] A second realization was that no matter what political, economic or social categories divide us, we humans are united in our insecurity before such forces. A third: one aspect of ensuring human continuity is psychological. Not only is our predicament self-created, but on the other side of the taboo against having thoughts or feelings about it lies the passion and psychic wisdom we need to mobilize for survival. Fourth: since both our insecurity and the task to survive are shared, addressing our unconscious and conscious relationship to them would best proceed, not in the relative isolation of the consulting room, but in the mutually supportive and empowering context of a group of people. I decided to dedicate myself to the task of providing such a context.

My first opportunity came in June. I was scheduled to give a plenary at a mental health conference. I wanted to design an experiential presentation that would affect participants on three levels. By raising their awareness of our situation, it would be educational. By crossing the taboo against showing feelings about our predicament, it would provide them with the basis for a model for human relationship in the nuclear age. Last, by exploring and hopefully making conscious their internal relationship to the situation, it would catalyze intrapsychic shifts and help them to grow as individuals and a group.

But there was a problem. Despite the fact that I had been planning and giving workshops and plenaries for years, I found this task a tall order. I was stumped. If, as social scientists and philosophers are saying, the nuclear age confronts Western peoples with the necessity for altering the very foundations of how we perceive life, death and human relations, the fact that the form of the plenary came to me in a dream is indicative. It suggests that what lies ahead for us may well exist at the edge of our collective consciousness. To call it forth is to open the doors to the unconscious and to integrate any guidance that passes the threshold into our conscious thinking, actions and goals.

Interestingly too, the form delivered in my dream was not a conventional group therapy or workshop session. It was a ritual. This development seemed noteworthy because, first of all, so many rituals provided by modern society have lost their abilities to teach, socialize and transform us; and second, because if we are to forge the kind of reconnection with our psyches, with each other and with our living planet that is our best hope for survival, we must create rituals that speak to us and through us of the peril, pain and promise of our times.

I called the plenary "Environmental Ritual."* Its form consisted of three concentric circles formed by the participants. The outer circle was the Circle of Information, a place for safe witnessing and reporting. The next circle was the Circle of Fear and Rage. The innermost one was the Circle of Sorrow. To begin, all participants were to stand in the outer circle. Any person could start by expressing a feeling or thought, personal or universal, about our common plight. "I have suffered for ten years with a disease I contracted from modern birth control." "My father was on the clean-up crew in Hiroshima and now he is dying of leukemia." "The *fish* in Lake Michigan have cancer!" "I feel scared all the time. I never know what new threat is going to surface and when it's going to hit *me.*" Then, to provide the all-important therapeutic affirmation of the truth of this statement, everyone in the circle would say: *"So It Is."* Since it is terrifying to confront our experience of living in the world today, we would then invoke a technique used, not in psychotherapy per se, but in religious practices the world over: to build bridges among ourselves and to that which is bigger than us all, we would chant, in this case *"Om"* or some agreed-upon song. Next a second participant would express a thought or feeling, and the ritual would proceed. The only requirement of participants was that each move to the circle that best reflected her or his current emotion, be that fear, anger, grief, calmness or observation.

The dream that presented this ritual was a synthesis of visual form and conceptual principle. The form of concentric circles is, of course, archtypal and can be found in nature and in nonlinear societies from Neolithic peoples to Native American cultures. The conceptual influences derived from my own interests and experience, but appropriately (and like the circles), they sprang from practices from around the globe. One was the work of thanatologist Elisabeth Kubler-Ross.[4], [5] Called

---

New Age Journal later renamed it "Ritual for Despair" (November 1980).

"griefwork," her approach to the psychology of death and dying is essentially an emotional passage past denial and through the loss, anger, depression, fear and sorrow that the prospect of dying elicits. By embarking upon and completing such a process, the dying and their loved ones can arrive at an acceptance of death—and a new sense of what it means to be alive. Like this process, the ritual provides the arena for participants to move beyond their denial of the possibility of collective death and express the very appropriate feelings about life and death, continuity and extinction, that they share.

One difference between facing individual death and this collective one is that in this larger situation we do not know the outcome. We do not know if more bombs will explode. We do not know how strong are the forces of life to counteract the poisons already spread around the globe from bomb-making, bomb-testing and unecological practices. We simply do not know. Another difference is that in this situation all people are facing the prospect of death simultaneously. The menace is a shared experience. According to therapeutic principle, as we face it together, we momentarily lose our sense of uniqueness, and our hitherto unexpressed experience is invoked, spoken, and acknowledged not alone, but in community. A final difference is that since this menace is human-made, the acceptance we then arrive at is *not* the acceptance of the inevitability of nuclear war or ecological disaster. It is the acceptance of the responsibility of each of us to do whatever we can to change the situation.

A second conceptual influence in the development of the ritual derived from the Chinese Revolution. This is "speaking bitterness," a practice used by peasants to heal the pain of past injustice and inspire creative participation in social change. An updated and Westernized version of this is feminist consciousness-raising. Both set up a conduit for individuals to deal with psychological problems caused by social realities. Both serve as interventions in the compensation and immobilization of individuals and as catalysts towards the development of a social awareness whose focus, community, and, hopefully, whose movement towards social change provides healing.

A last influence in the creation of the Environmental Ritual was my experience performing rituals in celebration of nature's cycles. Humans have always employed ritual as a therapeutic intervention into the cultural web of our psyches, and it has a long history of effecting personal support, perspective and well-being and social cohesiveness. Because the rituals I had been performing focused on the relationship of modern industrial people to nature, I had often seen sorrow, anger, fear and longing—but it was not until the Environmental Ritual that I linked the expression of these feelings with a process for harnessing them towards psychological awareness in the context of social change.

That morning in 1979, 150 people gathered in a rustic clearing for the experiment. I explained the origins, purpose and procedure of the ritual: I asked participants to speak their minds about what is happening to us because we live in the nuclear age. I also told them that although I was the one to instruct them in the procedure and to oversee and steer the process—the "therapist"—I would join them in speaking my mind too. Not only was my position in relation to the issue at hand no different from theirs, but accepted therapeutic principle tells us that in both individual psychotherapy and group process, a therapist/facilitator acknowledging her relationship to an issue and revealing her process can act as a guide.

After I spoke, hesitancy stilled each person standing in the circle. Expressing feelings about nuclear war or ecological disaster was an unheard-of thing to do. Beneath reluctant exteriors, though, they were ready. One stepped forward and announced that she had suffered a miscarriage she believed was caused by environmental pollution. Another said he'd been having nightmares about fallout shelters. A third called out to the group assembled that her mother had worked on atomic tests in Nevada, had eaten pork from live pigs roasted by a blast, and was now diseased. By the end of the two-hour session, 150 people were pounding their fists together, sobbing and holding one another. We felt outraged, afraid and sad, and as we realized how connected we are by the awful fate that hangs over us, a fourth circle spontaneously formed—one of kinship and commitment unlike any we had known before. The ritual completed itself when a woman placed her nine-month-old child in the center of the circle, and everyone held hands and sang songs of commitment and hope.

The Environmental Ritual is learnable, transmissible and flexible to different situations. Since 1979 it has been performed hundreds of times, helping thousands of people to cross the threshold from numbing, denial, rationalization, and repression, to stark acknowledgement of our predicament and their feelings about it. As I proceeded to develop and offer this experiment publicly, I discovered colleagues with similar ideas: Carol Wolman with Natalie Shiras, Kit Bricca and Joy Marcus, the earliest pioneers doing nuclear consciousness-raising groups; Joanna Macy exploring the spiritual aspects of the work; Harris Peck bringing his group therapy expertise to the issue; Fran Peavey, Barbara Hazard, and Kevin McVeigh applying their peer counseling skills; and Elissa Melamed her approach to personal empowerment. By 1981 a growing body of interrelated theory and practices was emerging, and the work came to be known as "despair and empowerment,"* "earthgrief,"** "waking up in the Nuclear Age,"*** "Day Before workshops,"**** "peace circles,"***** and "breaking through psychic numbing."******

These approaches rest on common ground. Perhaps the most important principle they share is the concept of direct confrontation: the psychological problems brought about by the nuclear menace are best addressed and our psychological potentials for averting disaster are best discovered by naming, acknowledging and feeling our emotions about them in a supportive, communal environment. Another principle they share is their integration of principles and practices from various disciplines, including psychology, religion and politics. Although no formal study has been made of the effects of such an approach, follow-up questionnaires and personal contacts with participants point towards some conclusions. Participation in the Environmental Ritual and related practices often catalyzes people to rethink their personal and social values. After one workshop a 35-year-old psychotherapist said that she learned "on a gut level" how precious each person is and how the sense of connection inspired by that insight is the most important state of mind for whatever action one might take to avert nuclear war or build a better world. This approach can also catalyze participants to take actions. After the first Environmental Ritual a previously uninvolved high school teacher went on to organize curricula on nuclear war and peace issues, first in her school and later in her district. A cellist founded an organization of classical musicians, put on benefit concerts for peace organizations, and played Russian and American music in Moscow and Washington. An administrator started a support group that went on to engage in civil disobedience against the development and deployment of nuclear weapons.

One Case: Some Implications for the Individual Client

This approach is also of interest because it can catalyze intrapsychic change and lead to personal growth. I was a witness to this aspect of the ritual because at the first performance of it, one client in my still-active practice was a participant. I am aware that in the annals of the therapist-client relationship, this situation was nontraditional—to some, even unheard-of. Yet there is justification for it. As Maxwell Jones has documented, nonhierarchical relationships can be psychotherapeutically effective when issues of common interest are addressed,[6] and there can be no argument that the issues raised by the Environmental Ritual were

---

*"Despair and empowerment" is the term first used by Joanna Macy and popularized by the national network of concerned activists, Interhelp.

**"Earthgrief" is the term used by Annie Prutzman.

***"Waking up in the Nuclear Age" is the term I have used through the organization of mental health professionals of the same name.

****"Day Before workshops" were organized and planned by Wendy Roberts and Claire Greensfelder after the ABC TV film *The Day After*.

*****"Peace circles" is the term used by Elissa Melamed.

******"Breaking through psychic numbing" is a widely used description that springs from the work of Robert Lifton.

of immediate and charged interest to both my client and myself.

At the time of this event Debby was 30 years old. We had been working together for six months. She was functioning, highly creative, emotionally expressive, and socially adept. A father's daughter, Debby had grown up with a professional father, a traditional mother and had sisters who were successful in a conventional sense as professionals, wives and mothers. She herself was in a long-term relationship that had lasted most of her adult life. It was unsatisfactory to her, though, and she felt powerless to change it or leave.

She was also depressive. In therapy she was working on issues of personal fragmentation—on the surface, between her different selves: the artist-creator of her own work, the therapist working with schizophrenics in a clinical setting, and the political organizer; and on a deeper level, between her father's values for her as either successful professional or housewife and her own less orthodox tendencies, what she called "the wrong path." She continually presented dream and visual material on themes of vulnerability and powerlessness, particularly in relation to men.

Because of her interest in the conference at which it took place, Debby also attended the Environmental Ritual. She participated in it fully, emoting with passion and telling the group about the pain and confusion of her life. Although the content of what she shared was similar to what she often said in therapy sessions, there were two differences. One I have already mentioned: for the first time she was witnessing me, her therapist, as a fellow participant with feelings about our mutual predicament not unlike her own.* Secondly, although we had brought in a wider perspective on her personal problems in our sessions, the ritual was the first time Debby clearly and without hesitation set her problems in a socio-historical context. This effect has likewise been referred to in the literature of group therapy. For instance, Harris Peck has shown that group settings can have a positive impact on individual perception and competence.[7]

At our next session, Debby described the ritual as a "revelation." She had been "deeply involved in my personal metaphor," she explained, and at the ritual "all this hit the universal pool. I didn't feel crazy anymore. I saw I was part of something bigger. Even though I know I have to take responsibility for improving my life, for the first time I understood that I wasn't to blame—and I wasn't alone."

After this, Debby's life and therapy took a turn. In our work she focused more attention on her relationship with her father, and after some months she decided to leave her unsatisfactory love relationship

---

*I am not recommending that therapists and clients participate in this kind of experience together as part of their work. Rather I am indicating that my presence at this event was part of Wendy's shift in perception.

and move out on her own. She also entertained glimpses of her work and political interests as more integrated, saying that doing therapy was indeed political because "to empower anybody, anywhere in this society, is political." New energy also infused her studio work. She began a series of sculptures she saw as a political—and healing—statement. These were tall standing women in the vulnerable process of giving birth—to unformed, incomplete rocks and eggs, or perhaps to their own maimed guts. Yet the women also had a noble quality and a sense of strength. She described them as "people taking a stand in a fragile world."

Psychotherapy in the Nuclear Age: New Horizons

One aspect of the challenge that presents itself to us in these times exists on the psychological plane. As mental health professionals, it behooves us to apply our knowledge, methodology and skills to this challenge—yet psychology as it is traditionally defined is not broad enough to encompass the whole of our task. For one thing, psychotherapy in the traditional clinical setting cannot offer the kind of help individuals need to address the psychological problems effected by the threat of universal disaster of nuclear war or ecological catastrophe. For another, the challenge of our times calls us to respond with every resource we have and from every level of our being—and so to synthesize practices and principles previously categorized into distinct, isolated disciplines. We need new approaches that can build bridges among the individual, family, nation and global community, and between the rational and intuitive aspects of ourselves. The Environmental Ritual is one such approach that has shown itself to be useful to educate and activate participants and also, as in the case of Debby, to contribute to some individuals' personal growth.

In recent years many mental health professionals have begun to respond to the challenges of the nuclear age, and there are today several hundred people and a number of professional organizations contributing to this field. "Taking a stand in a fragile world" is what psychology and psychotherapy are beginning to do—as we as professionals widen their concern to include areas not traditionally considered part of their terrain and as we offer new and relevant forums for human transformation.

REFERENCES

1.   Robert Jay Lifton, *The Broken Connection*. N.Y.: Simon and Schuster, 1979.
2.   William Beardslee and John Mack, "The Impact of Nuclear Developments on Children and Adolescents." In *Psycho-Social Aspects of Nuclear Developments,* Task Force Report 20. Washington, D.C.: American Psychiatric Association, 1982.
3.   Benina Gould, et al., "Children and the Threat of Nuclear War." *Therapy Now,* Summer 1984.

4. Elisabeth Kubler-Ross, *On Death and Dying.* N.Y.: Macmillan, 1969.
5. Elisabeth Kubler-Ross, *Death: Final Stage of Growth.* Englewood Cliffs, N.J.: Prentice-Hall, 1975.
6. Maxwell Jones, *Therapeutic Community: A New Treatment Method in Psychiatry.* N.Y.: Basic Books, 1953.
7. Harris Peck, "Some Relationships Between Group Process and Mental Health Phenomena in Theory and Practice." *International Journal of Group Psychotherapy,* Volume XIII, Number 3, 1963.

BIOGRAPHICAL NOTES

Ellen Becker, M.A. is a founding member of Psychotherapists for Social Responsibility, and has led nuclear workshops in the United States and Canada. She is a psychotherapist in private practice in Oakland, California.

Lloyd deMause is Director of the Institute of Psychohistory, founder of the Journal of Psychohistory, and teaches at the New York Center for Psychoanalytic Training and the City University of New York. He is the author of numerous books, including *Foundations of Psychohistory* and *Reagan's America,* and is recognized as the founder of the discipline of psychohistory.

Wolfgang Giegerich, Ph.D. is a lecturer and training analyst at the C.G. Jung Institute, Stuttgart, Germany, where he is also in the private practice of Jungian psychoanalysis. He is the founding editor of *Gorgo—Zeitschrift fur archetypische Psychologie und bildhaftes Denken,* has lectured at the Eranos Conferences, Switzerland, and has more than 30 publications in German, American, Italian, and, in the near future, Japanese handbooks and professional journals.

Chellis Glendinning, Ph.D. is a Fellow at Peace and Common Security Institute (PACS) in San Francisco, a co-founder of the international network Interhelp, and the author of *Waking Up in the Nuclear Age,* (William Morrow, 1987). Dr. Glendinning also serves on the Community Advisory Board of Peace and Conflict Studies Department, University of California at Berkeley.

Joanna Macy, Ph.D. is the best-known of the many practitioners of despair and empowerment work. In the last decade she has led hundreds of workshops throughout the world. She holds a doctorate in religion, and is the author of two books, *Dharma and Development: Religion as Resource in the Sarvodaya Self-Help Movement,* and *Despair and Empowerment in the Nuclear Age.*

Paul Olsen, Ph.D. is Director of Publications at the National Institute for the Psychotherapies, New York City, where he is also Co-Director of the Nuclear Education Project. He is general editor of two book series, *New Directions in Psychotherapy* and *Perspectives in Psychotherapy,* and editor of the journal *Comprehensive Psychotherapy.* He has published three critically-acclaimed novels, numerous short stories, and several non-fiction books on psychology and social issues.

Kenneth Porter, M.D. is Assistant Clinical Professor of Psychiatry at Columbia College of Physicians and Surgeons, Attending Psychiatrist at St. Luke's-Roosevelt Hospital, and a leader in Physicians for Social Responsibility. He is in the private practice of psychiatry in New York City.

Deborah Rinzler, Ph.D. is Co-Director of the Nuclear Education Project of the National Institute for the Psychotherapies, New York City, where she is also special supervisor in sensory awareness. She is in clinical practice of psychotherapy and sensory awareness in New York City.

Adela G. Wilkeson, M.D. is a psychiatrist on the staff of McLean Hospital in Belmont, Mass. and is engaged in the private practice of psychiatry.